To Hell with Sickness

by Bill Prankard

Belleville, Ontario, Canada

To Hell with Sickness

First printing December 2004
Second printing August 2005

Library and Archives Canada Cataloguing in Publication

Prankard, Bill, 1945-
To Hell with sickness / Bill Prankard.

Includes bibliographical references.
ISBN 1-55306-871-8

1. Prankard, Bill, 1945- 2. Spiritual healing. 3. Healing--Religious aspects--Christianity. I. Title.

BT732.5.P734 2004 234'.131 C2004-907148-3

For more information, please contact:
Bill Prankard
Bill Prankard Evangelistic Association,
Box 7007, Station V, Ottawa, ON K1L 8E2
www.bpea.com

Guardian Books is an imprint of *Essence Publishing,* a Christian Book Publisher dedicated to furthering the work of Christ through the written word. For more information, contact: 20 Hanna Court, Belleville, Ontario, Canada K8P 5J2. Phone: 1-800-238-6376 • Fax: (613) 962-3055.
publishing@essencegroup.com • www.essencegroup.com

Table of Contents

Introduction

Where does sickness come from?

Did God send sickness to test us?

How do I know if it is God's will to heal me?

Does God anoint only a special few with the gift of healing?

Sincere Christians ask me questions like this regularly. It concerned me that there seems to be so little understanding about divine healing among believers today. Then I realized it's because there is actually a drought of teaching on the subject.

Jesus said, in John 8:32, "*You will know the **truth**, and the **truth** will set you free*" (NIV, emphasis added). If you are not aware of the truth of God's Word concerning healing, how can you expect to be set free from the condition that plagues you?

Good teachers relate to people; they help you grasp the message they are trying to communicate. Jesus is the greatest teacher that ever walked the earth. People flocked to hear Him teach because they could easily understand His message. He conveyed deep truths in a manner everyone could readily comprehend.

When He spoke to farmers, He used vocabulary they could relate to, using examples and terminology associated with farming. When He spoke to fishermen, he did the same. Even children understood His message, because He explained everything to them simply, through parables and stories.

Many Christians say they are looking for "*deep*" teaching. They attend Bible conferences and seminars regularly, listening to complex intellectual sermons. Often they return from these events totally overwhelmed, saying, "Wow, that was *deep* teaching!" In reality, they are saying, "I didn't understand a word!"

That kind of teaching doesn't reach hearts and transform lives. The simple truth of God's Word will!

Receiving from God shouldn't be complicated. Sadly, the Church over the last two thousand years has turned the simple message of Jesus' miracle-working power into a complex and often times perplexing philosophy.

The majority of people today don't believe they could ever have a meaningful relationship with God or receive from Him, because somehow the Church has failed to relate to them. It's time to get back to the simplicity and clarity of the true message of the Bible: "Jesus loves you and wants to give you His best!"

Know the truth, and let it set you free, spiritually, physically and emotionally! It's that easy!

In the following pages, I want to take you on a simple biblical journey of faith—a journey that will lead you to your miracle.

Bill Prankard

Chapter One

God Is Big; the Devil Is Small

"Teach the basics." That's what I felt God speak to my heart one day a few years ago when I was in prayer.

Nobody has ever mistaken me for a great theological professor, expounding on the deep mysteries of God's Word, so I was a little taken aback by what I felt God saying to me. "Teach the basics?" I thought I had been. My teachings were never complicated, and I always made every effort to speak plainly, so I answered Him and said, "But God, I am teaching the basics."

"Tell the people that I am big."

"But Lord, they know that," I answered.

"Tell the people that I am big and the devil is small. Look at the Church. They say that I'm big, but they live like I'm little. They say the devil is small, but they live like he is big. They live in fear of him as though he were bigger than I am."

This conversation was, as I said, a few years ago. Since that time, I am happy to report, many believers are beginning to shift their thinking, and as a result, their attitudes are changing. They are beginning to get hold of the fact that they serve a powerful God who loves them and wants to give them good things. At the same time, they are beginning to realize their authority as children of the King and the power given to them to ward off the attacks of the enemy.

In John 10:10, Jesus says, "*The thief does not come except to steal, and to kill, and to destroy. I have come that they may have life, and that they may have it more abundantly.*"

In this passage, Jesus refers to the devil as a thief. A thief steals. The devil always takes—he never gives. He will tell you he'll give you peace, pleasure and freedom. Many people get caught up in his lies and fall for his trap and temptations, such as "Don't be so old fashioned," "If it feels good, do it," and "Don't be a holier-than-thou person." But because he is a thief and a liar, listening to his lines will only lead you to become spiritually, emotionally and physically bankrupt.

Jesus told the story of the prodigal son. It's the story of a young man who felt restricted by the rules and responsibilities imposed on him by his father. In his mind, his ungodly friends were enjoying life far more than he was. He thought that he could find true fulfillment if he could just have the money and the freedom to pursue his own path in life.

His father didn't stop him. Instead, he gave his son his inheritance. The young man began a life of wild living and immorality, squandering his fortune and breaking his father's heart.[1]

In the same way, God won't stop us from "doing our own thing." He's given us free will. We can choose whether or not to pursue the enemy's lies, but at what cost? The Bible tells us that *"There is a way that seems right to a man, But its end is the way of death."*[2]

After losing all his money, his friends and his self-respect, the young man came to his senses. He realized that he had fallen for a lie, that rebellion hadn't brought him any of the things he thought it would. He began to remember all that he had once possessed, and he came to the conclusion that everything he had ever wanted or needed was back in his father's house. It was there that he had enjoyed security, provision, acceptance and forgiveness. True happiness was there.

You and I can follow the enemy's enticements, believing that will bring fulfillment, but, just like the prodigal son, eventually we'll discover the Source of real fulfillment—in the Father's house.

A while ago, I met a couple with a three-year-old daughter. The husband was doing very well in his career while his wife pursued a university degree. Their little girl was growing up, and everything seemed to be going well for them. All of a sudden, and literally out of the blue, the mother was hit with a serious, crippling disease. She could no longer study or go to school. Her career was put on hold. Because of the seriousness of the condition, her husband had to leave his employment to look after her. Before long their savings were depleted and their finances strained, because so much of her treatment was not covered by insurance. This young lady's illness stole their dreams. I looked at the little girl and learned that for about two of her three years of life her mother had not been able to hold and play with her. That's the devil! He steals, kills and destroys.

The enemy is a lying thief who gives the illusion that listening to him will bring freedom and fulfillment. Ask an addict why she ever started experimenting with drugs. Ask an alcoholic what he thought he would gain by drowning himself in drink. Ask any young man or woman who has given in to sexual urges outside of marriage why they ever agreed to such a relationship. They will all tell you that they thought they would get "something good" out of it. Basically, they gave in to the enemy's cruel lies.

Don't Be Nice to the Devil!

Canadians have a reputation for being "nice." We've been brought up to be polite, and that's good. But as believers, oftentimes we try to be nice even to the devil! He is a defeated foe, and *"He who is in you is greater than he who is in the world."*[3] Rob Critchley's song "Great Big God, Little Bitty Devil!"[4] says it well.

Our God is a ***big*** God! Yes, there is a devil and there are demons. But let us not get too focused on them, because we know our God is stronger, mightier and far more able!

When we constantly talk about the enemy and his works, we are magnifying him, making him seem bigger than he is. That allows fear to creep in. But we have been called to magnify our Lord. He has given us authority over the enemy. It is important that we understand who we are in Christ.

David recognized the bigness of God. When he saw Goliath in action and saw the fear he'd brought on the people of God, he became angry. He knew there was something wrong with that picture. *"Who is this uncircumcised*

Philistine, that he should defy the armies of the living God?"[5] In other words, David was saying, "Who does this puny enemy think he is? Our God is so much bigger than him!" When the people of God are paralyzed by fear or hindered by sickness and disease, there is something wrong. Oftentimes, God puts dreams and goals in the hearts of certain people, but they cannot fulfill these dreams because of physical weakness. It's not God who prevents the fulfillment of these dreams. He's the one who gave them in the first place! He does not call someone and then hinder that person from answering the call.

Why is it that so many people fear the devil or give him what they call a "healthy respect"? Christians have often cautioned me to be careful when speaking of the enemy in case I might somehow upset him and provoke some sort of retaliation.

I was speaking in a church recently when I made a few comments about the devil. I believe my exact words were " We're gonna kick the devil's face in!" It didn't take long for the pastor to confront me after the service. "Maybe you should just tone some of that down. We had another speaker here who made a lot of negative comments about the devil, and he got sick. We just don't want to upset anything."

I stood there absolutely stunned. "Tone it down"? "We don't want to upset anything"? How on earth did the Church, the Body of Christ, arrive at such a defensive, timid posture? The four Gospels tell me that Jesus was anything but defensive. He came here on a mission, and that mission was to destroy the works of the enemy! Heaven launched a massive offensive assault by sending the Son of God to earth in the form of a man. The book of Acts and the rest of the New Testament document the aggressive advance of the Church, with souls being added daily.[6]

So where did we go wrong? At what point in Church history did we make a wrong turn? It is time for the Church to once again stand up, take her rightful place of God-given authority, turn from her defensive state and position herself for attack. No longer can we afford to concern ourselves with "not upsetting the devil" or taking on a "politically correct" attitude towards him. We are called to do severe damage to the kingdom of darkness. Each one of us is called to become Satan's personal nightmare!

"But I'm comfortable with my life right now; why would I want to stir things up by declaring war on the devil?" you ask.

There is a fundamental flaw in this type of thinking. The simple fact of the matter is that if we are truly followers of Christ, we have, by default, become an enemy of hell.

The Church has often been referred to as a "sleeping giant," a complacent, lethargic body of lukewarm believers. America didn't believe it was at war prior to the attack of 9/11 either, but that didn't change the fact that she had an enemy who had declared war on her! How many times in the moments and days following the tragic events of that day did we hear the U.S. referred to as a "sleeping giant"?

The Church is in the same situation as the people of God were in when Goliath threatened them. They knew that they were the people of God and were standing against an ungodly nation. They knew God was on their side. And yet, they were concentrating so much on the giant enemy that they were paralyzed. Someone had to remind them that they were the people of the living God, that this giant could do nothing to them.

David was angry. He faced the enemy with courage and shouted,

> *"You come to me with a sword, with a spear, and with a javelin. But I come to you in the name of the* LORD *of hosts, the God of the armies of Israel, whom you have defied. This day the* LORD *will deliver you into my hand, and I will strike you and take your head from you. And this day I will give the carcasses of the camp of the Philistines to the birds of the air and the wild beasts of the earth, that all the earth may know that there is a God in Israel."*[7]

In plain English, David was saying, "Enough is enough! You have intimidated and laughed at the people of God for the last time! You are going down!"

It is time for the Church to rise up and say, "Enough is enough!"

Whatever steals, kills and destroys is not from God but from the enemy. Sickness steals, kills and destroys, so it cannot be a gift from God.

Some people may say, "Oh, but my sickness forced me to stay in bed for weeks and do nothing but read the Bible. It helped me grow deeper in God." Of course, God can bring wonderful things out of terrible situations, but that does not mean that those situations come from God. God can take a curse and turn it into blessing, but that does not mean that He is the author of the curse.

God Wants Us to Enjoy Life!

The enemy is relentless. He will constantly try to put thoughts of fear in our minds or attack us in various ways, in order to steal, kill and destroy. In contrast, Jesus says, "*I have come that they may have life, and that they may have it more abundantly.*"[8]

Jesus' entire reason for coming is summed up in this one verse. He came to give life—not just an ordinary, mundane existence but life "*more abundantly.*" It goes against every religious thought in the world—God actually wants you to enjoy life and have fun. All the things He's created for us are for our delight, to enjoy!

You are not having abundant life if you don't have any money and can't pay your bills.

You are not having abundant life if you are sick and your body is racked with pain.

You are not having abundant life if you are empty and dark inside.

Jesus came to give you life, in your spirit, soul and body—and life more abundantly!

When I was growing up, I was led to believe that being a Christian was something to be endured, not enjoyed. One Sunday morning while sitting with my family in church, my foot began instinctively tapping along as the organist played a hymn during the offering. My mother, noticing the foot, slapped my arm and scolded me, saying, "Stop it! You're in church!"

I got the message. An emotional response of any kind was considered sacrilegious. On the other hand, quietness and order was reverence.

I think that's why it's often so hard for people from religious backgrounds similar to mine to enjoy freedom. It appears sacrilegious, because of the way they've been programmed. I came to realize that kind of thinking has nothing to do with Jesus. It is just a man-made tradition.

George McMurtry, a church administrator from Bangor, Ireland, received an amazing miracle in 2000. I'll never forget that Tuesday night service in Toronto I was ministering in. It was a great meeting; the presence of God had filled the place, and people started receiving healings. One of the words of knowledge God gave me was that somebody's hand was being healed.

I had never met George, but I learned later that he had come to Canada with some of the leaders of his church to be in the conference where I was ministering. Because of the devastating results of five strokes he'd suffered (some so serious that the doctor felt he would not survive), he had been forced to leave his job. Even after all the treatment, therapy and medication, he was left totally paralyzed down one side, his left leg withered to about half the size of his right leg and his left arm curled up to his chest, lifeless and useless as well. The doctors had told him that this was the best it was going to get and that he'd never get better.

He couldn't work. He couldn't function without constant care. He couldn't contribute to his family's well-being or to the life of the church family he loved.

Sickness had stolen his life from him. It had killed his hope. In fact, he admitted later that at times he wondered if it would be better if he just died so that he wouldn't have to continue enduring his condition and wouldn't be a burden to his wife and family.

Sickness had destroyed his hope for the future. He had no guarantee that another stroke wouldn't end what little life remained and faced the prospect of never being "normal" again.

With the help of a leg brace, a cane and his friends, he managed to make the trip from Ireland to Canada to attend the conference. When the word went forward that someone's hand was being healed, his withered hand started moving. Then his arm started moving.

His friends saw what was happening and cried out, "George, you better go up to the front and testify." As he quickly made his way up the aisle, he heard his friends calling, "Hey, George, you forgot your cane!" He realized that he didn't need it! As he walked, the brace, held together by Velcro straps, began to come loose. When he checked to see why, he realized his leg had returned to its normal size and had regained its full function!

I was told afterwards that he is a rather conservative man. But as he made his way to the front of the auditorium, he was jumping, crying and laughing. I called his friends forward, and they verified what he was saying. As I watched him jump and dance around, I felt the Spirit of God telling me that I was watching someone come into abundant life. He was just starting to live. Until then, George hadn't been living—he had just been surviving.

When he returned to Ireland, his doctor performed every possible test and declared that George was totally healed. He remarked that George's amazing recovery had nothing to do with any medical intervention and said, "We must give all the glory to God."

George not only resumed his full workload as administrator at his church but took on several other responsibilities as well. God received much glory because of George's healing. The front page of the secular newspaper in Bangor, Ireland, did a three-quarter- page article, complete with full-colour photos of George McMurtry's miraculous healing. He ministers in scores of churches and lays that restored hand, filled with healing anointing, on the sick—and sees them recover, too. That's abundant life. And it is a kick in the devil's face!

God is the Giver of good gifts, and healing is a good gift.

Sickness is a bad "gift." It cannot come from God, because He does not give bad things. He is not bad. He cannot give sickness, because He does not have sickness. If you have even the slightest notion that sickness is something that God gives to people, you're going to have difficulty believing for a miracle, and you most certainly will not have a successful healing ministry to others.

Sickness steals. Sickness kills. Sickness destroys. It comes from the *thief*, the devil. He will try to make you accept his "gift" of sickness. But, as God's child, you can stand your ground and say, "No! I will not accept it! Sickness, go back to hell where you came from!"

---

[1] Luke 15:11-32.

[2] Proverbs 16:25.

[3] 1 John 4:4.

[4] Robert Critchley, *Great Big God* (Wild Ox Publishing, 1997).

[5] 1 Samuel 17:26.

[6] Acts 2:47.

[7] 1 Samuel 17:45,46.

[8] John 10:10.

Chapter Two

Paid in Full

No More Curse!

In Genesis chapter 3, we read of mankind's original sin in the Garden of Eden; we've come to know it as "the fall." A curse came over the earth and on all mankind as the consequence of man's disobedience to God.

The curse was made up of three parts.

1. *Sickness*

God created a perfect world, a world without sickness, death or disease. He never intended for humans to be sick or to have pain.

Try to imagine somehow being transported back in time to visit Adam as he enjoyed all the provisions and pleasure of the Garden of Eden, before sin entered. Perhaps we'd say,

"I'm really having a lot of pain from my arthritis today." Adam would respond, "What is pain? What is arthritis?" He wouldn't have a clue what these things are. They enjoyed perfection—no sin, no sickness, no want.

Man's sin and the resulting curse, however, changed all that. Sickness became a part of the human experience because of the curse.

2. *Poverty*

God delights in blessing His children; He always has. Adam and Eve were blessed beyond measure. They had everything they would ever want, never needing anything or having to go without. They were prosperous in the truest sense of the word. The one thing—the only thing—they were asked not to touch was the one thing that would bring the curse.

Our daughter Margie's first words were "No, no, Margie." When she began toddling around the house, we decided we weren't going to overly "babyproof" our home, other than putting away things that might harm her. Instead, whenever she tried to grab something that was off limits, we'd say, 'No, no, Margie." One day we saw her standing in the living room with her finger very close to something she wasn't supposed to touch, talking to herself and saying, "No, no, Margie!" She had heard the phrase so often it was the first thing she learned to say.

In the same way, Adam and Eve knew the rules. They knew that God had given them the abundance of the entire Garden for their provision and enjoyment. But He instructed them not to eat the fruit of the tree of knowledge of good and evil. By yielding to sin, Adam and Eve brought a curse upon themselves—a curse that included the loss of prosperity. They began to be in want for the first time.

3. *Death*

Man died that day in the garden. Adam and Eve died spiritually, and the process of physical death began as well.

God created everything with such a wonderful beginning, and man wrecked it. God didn't wreck it; we did. The love of God was such that even after mankind messed up His perfect plan, He stood in the garden and made a way to fix it.

That's the good news! When Jesus came to this world in the form of a man, he took the curse upon Himself. He paid the price for us to be free from sickness, poverty and death. Because of the cross, we can enjoy health, strength, provision and abundant life. The moment we turn to Jesus, abundant life begins. We don't have to wait for heaven! It is available to us right now.

The heart of the Father is amazing. He wanted a friend—someone to talk with and walk with, someone who would choose to love Him. That's the heart of God. He has promised to come and take us to where He is, just so that we can be with Him. The curse man lives under is in no way a reflection on God's nature. Man decided to not believe His Word, and whenever we decide to disregard the Word of God, we're going to run into trouble. We place ourselves under the influence of the curse. Sickness comes from the pit of hell. It's a result of the curse.

Death has lost its sting! For a Christian, death is not a bad thing. The Apostle Paul knew that; that's why he said, *"For to me, to live is Christ, and to die is gain."*[1] We have an amazing reward waiting for us in heaven. Death holds no fear!

I do, however, have a hard time accepting that Christians should die of sickness and disease; I have a hard time accepting that Christians need to give in to sickness and accept it as a natural result of the ageing process.

If you, as a born-again, Bible-believing, blood-bought Christian, are going to die, then you should die of old age, not of disease. How much better would it be to just simply pass from this life to the next! It worked for Enoch, Moses, and Elijah, and we can expect it to work for us.

I like the way Moses died. He climbed a mountain and disappeared. His body was never found.[2] Better yet, Elijah didn't even die! He went up to heaven in a whirlwind of glory.[3] And Enoch simply went for a walk with the Lord one day, and never came back![4]

I was told by an elderly woman not long ago, "Well, at my age, I have to expect aches and pains." I do not accept that at all! It most certainly wasn't the case with Moses. At the age of 120, he had the strength of a young man. Even his eyesight was still good![5] If Moses at 120 was the picture of health, then I believe you can be too! You can expect to walk in divine health.

It's time for the Church of Jesus Christ to declare war on sickness, pain and disease! As reasonable as it sounds, there is nothing biblical about holding the hand of the person suffering from illness, encouraging them to accept their lot and die. It is time for us to become unreasonable! That's the message my wife and I have been bringing to churches across the country for over thirty years. Be totally unreasonable!

It's time to tell sickness, "Go to hell!"

All That, For Me?

In 1 Corinthians 6:20 we read, "*For you were bought at a price; therefore glorify God* ***in your body*** *and in your* *spirit, which are God's"* (emphasis added). The price has been paid for your healing!

Galatians 3:13 says, *"Christ has redeemed us from the curse of the law, having become a curse for us (for it is written, 'Cursed is everyone who hangs on a tree')."* Man's sin allowed the curse to come upon this earth, bringing sickness, poverty and death. Jesus redeemed us from the curse.

This is something we know. It's in our heads, but it needs to get into our hearts.

In essence, the devil kidnapped us. He held us in bondage to sin, sickness and poverty. There was a ransom put on our lives. We needed to be redeemed.

A thought went through my mind once, so I asked my wife, Gwen, "Honey, if I was kidnapped, how much would you pay to get me back?" She didn't want to answer and quickly changed the subject. The question lingered in my mind, so I did what I've learned always works better; I asked her the same question when we were in public. I decided that if I asked her the question in a service, she'd have to answer—and I'd re-phrase it so she wouldn't even know it was the same question.

The moment came one evening when, in the midst of my message, I stepped down from the platform and asked, "Gwen, if someone kidnapped me and contacted you saying that you could have me back provided you paid them five million dollars in twenty-four hours, what would you do?"

Without hesitating, she said, "Please give him this message: 'Have a nice life.'" Then she just smiled. She assured me it wasn't because she didn't love me or wouldn't want me back; she just knew it was a ridiculous scenario and that nobody would ever expect her to come up with that much money. Most of us couldn't.

There is a reason that very rich and famous people have security. Criminals know that if they kidnap a member of their families, it's very possible for them to get millions of dollars within a very short time. They'd have the ability to pay the ransom.

According to Galatians 3:13, we were taken hostage by the enemy, and a ransom demand was placed on our lives. The most expensive price ever asked for anything was asked for you. All the silver and gold and all the wealth in the world wasn't enough to pay it. There wasn't a person on earth able to pay the price.

The devil is bad. Man was hopeless, helpless and unworthy to free himself from Satan's bondage. But God is good! Jesus saw our condition and knew the price that must be paid. Because of His great love, and because His nature gave Him the ability to redeem us, He said, "They have great value. I'll pay the price. They are worth it."

That is the gospel message. That's the reason for the cross. When we were held hostage and a ransom placed on our lives, we needed to be rescued and redeemed. Jesus paid the price. He became the curse. He was the only one who could, because He had no sin. He was the only one who could pay the price and redeem us from the curse—and He did!

Let me warn you; the devil is going to try to convince you that you're not worth very much and not very valuable—that you can't do very much. You must know that the enemy is wrong! With God's help, there's nothing you can't do. Jesus gave us His power over sickness.[6] He told us to speak to it and tell it to go away.[7] You'll be more effective in your ministry to the sick if you speak with authority to the sickness and pain and tell it to go back to hell, where it came from!

Paul recognized that he could do nothing of significance in his own strength. Without God, we can't do anything. But we aren't without Him! Philippians 4:13 says, *"I can do all things through Christ who strengthens me."* We may not feel worthy, but it has nothing to do with us. Jesus paid the price and gave us His power to defeat Satan's assaults, including sickness. Through Him, we've been made worthy to receive all of God's good gifts.[8]

The enemy will try to attack your sense of worth, but stand your ground!

I'm sure every preacher in the world has said what I say when I invite people to receive Christ and the wonderful life He has for them. I tell them that if they had been the only one, Jesus still would have come and done all He did. I've always believed that. But an experience I had in the Russian Arctic a few years ago really demonstrated it clearly to me.

It was our team's first summer mission there. We had always gone in the winter, because the Nenets, the Eskimo people we are trying to reach, are nomadic, living in tents and following their migrating reindeer herds. During the summer, the herds head far up into the northern tundra, away from civilization. But in the winter months, some of them come far enough south that they're more accessible. It's still far above the Arctic Circle and under extreme conditions, but from where our workers live on the edge of the tundra, it's about twenty-five to fifty miles to some of these people. Travelling by snow machine, tank vehicle, helicopter or reindeer sleigh, it is a relatively short journey on the tundra to find them.

Getting to these people is difficult, but harvesting isn't. One man said to us, "We've been waiting for you. We knew there was a God, but we just didn't know how to get to

Him. We go out of our tents at night and look up at the stars and moon and call out to the sky, 'Whoever you are, send somebody to tell us how to get to you.'"

The people of this region are the most expensive souls in the world. To fly just one of our team members from Baffin Island (Canada's Arctic) to Toronto, where the team meets for the mission, costs thousands of dollars—and that's just the beginning of the trip! From Toronto, the whole team has to fly to Moscow, then continue up to the most northern city in the Russian Arctic accessible by plane. From there we join our Russian workers and set out on land across the tundra.

The real challenge, however, is getting through all the red tape in Russia. A lot of these areas are closed military zones, where nuclear testing and other classified operations take place. Very few people are allowed to travel there. But because our team usually includes Canadian Inuit members, the officials see our work as a "cultural exchange" and tend to be somewhat lenient.

The challenge I was having on this summer mission was that very few Nenets had come south. Most of them were far up along the coast. I kept feeling that we needed to reach more, but our Russian workers kept telling me it was impossible to get there. But God kept telling me to go. I sent a message over and told them we were coming in the summer and we had to find a way to go farther.

I got a message back that they had found a tank. It used to be a military tank, but now it was privately owned. They said it could go anywhere. The tank would pull a second compartment that has bunk beds and a stove, to serve as our living quarters. This tank goes across the tundra, through rivers and over mountains. It's absolutely amazing.

We bumped along over the tundra, searching for these

nomadic people who travel in single-family units. There are no maps to tell you where to find them, because they change location almost every week. They take down their tents and move as the reindeer move.

In each tent we came upon, we found people who had never heard the gospel message but were open to hearing the Good News. We told them God loves them and wants to save them and heal them. They accepted it readily. It made sense to them that if God is good and loves them, then He wants to give them eternal life and heal them.

I was prepared to minister to small numbers on this particular trip. I knew we would be ministering to just one family at a time. But at one point in the mission we had been travelling all day in the tank, which wasn't much fun, persevering hour after hour but seeing no tents, no people, and no indication that anyone was camping in the region.

Finally, towards the end of the day, we spotted a tent and headed towards it. One man came out of the tent, so we asked him about his family. He explained that the family was about twenty miles away over the hills. He was alone, tending the family's herd of a thousand reindeer. Occasionally one of the other family members would come and relieve him and he'd go back, but this day he was alone. We had a wonderful team and had spent a lot of time, effort and money to get there. So I started thinking, "We can't waste our time here. We'd better go find the family."

Just then, one of our Russian missionary workers asked me, "Shall we serve the one?" I realized the answer wasn't "No." The answer was "Yes, that's what Jesus would do." So I turned to one of our Canadian Inuit leaders, David Aglukark, and said, "Go get your guitar. We're going to have a service."

Here in North America, success in ministry is often measured in numbers. The larger the crowd you can attract, the more successful you are considered to be. God has a different way of judging success, but that's how we often see it.

We had an entire service for a congregation of one. The Inuit leaders sang and shared their testimonies as well as their culture. They talked about how, as children, they had been raised in igloos. The man just sat there and looked at them. They told him what Jesus had done in their homes and families in northern Canada.

When they were all finished, I asked my associate, Bruce Alexander, to share the gospel. (I was glad the man didn't slip out of the service, because we sure would have noticed!) After giving a simple salvation message and telling how he had found Christ, Bruce gave an altar call.

It may have been the smallest meeting we ever had, but it was by far the most successful. One hundred percent of the crowd got saved that day! He really got saved. His countenance changed. His eyes lit up. He began to laugh.

Our Russian worker looked at the man and asked, "Have you ever heard this before? Has anyone ever told you about Jesus?"

He answered, "No—this is the first time."

Through the interpreter, I told him, "You must be very valuable to God that He would bring us all the way from the other side of the world for you." As I spoke, I felt the Holy Spirit say to me, "If this was the only man out here—if there were no other tents or families—I still would have had you come and spend all the money, travel all these miles and go through all the red tape."

Wow! We know in our heads that we're valuable to God, but after seeing it first-hand, I realized that if this man was that important to God, then so was I. And so are you. We need to understand the value God places on our lives; then we'll understand the full meaning of Galatians 3:13.

I was trying to process all of this on the plane going home. Reading through the Gospels, things that I've read for years suddenly jumped out at me like never before. Jesus was in Judea but decided to go to Galilee. To get there, *"He needed to go through Samaria."*[9] It wasn't because travelling through Samaria was necessarily the quickest route to Galilee or that there would be huge crowds waiting for him there; on the contrary, there was one woman who would meet Him at the well—a woman whom no one else would talk to.

Another time He was going through Jericho, with huge crowds gathered around. He stopped at a tree and spoke to one man. The Scriptures say he was passing through Jericho, but He changed His agenda and decided to stay there.[10] He went to Zacchaeus's house to bring him salvation. That's Jesus.

Ministry isn't about masses. Ministry is touching one life at a time. Jesus was on the shores of Galilee with a crowd gathered around. He turned to his disciples and said, "Let's get in the boat and go to the other side."[11] Why? Because there was a man named Legion that needed to be delivered.

Jesus puts great value on people that our society doesn't value at all. I find that really encouraging! You are important to Almighty God. You are of great value to Him. God considered you worth every drop of blood He shed, every beating He took and the humiliation He endured.

The experience with the man on the tundra changed me. It changed my ministry. It changed my attitude. My attitude about crowds and numbers has changed. I have come to appreciate, more than ever, the value of one soul.

The first time I went to Calcutta, India, Mark Buntain, a great man of God who has since passed away, introduced me to Mother Teresa. Mother Teresa, a Catholic nun, and Mark Buntain, a Pentecostal minister, worked together, caring for the poorest of the poor—sick people who could not afford hospital expenses. Mother Teresa was an amazing lady who taught me a great deal by example. She loved Jesus, and the magnitude of her ministry around the world was phenomenal.

I ministered in Calcutta five or six times and had several opportunities to visit with her. During one such visit I asked her, "Did you ever expect that God was going to use you in such a big way?"

She said to me, "Well, when I was a girl in school, I really was the least of the least. Any girl in my class could have done more than I did. They had more ability, more talent and more things going for them. But I just gave my life to Jesus and began loving and helping people as I saw their need. There's no such thing as a big ministry. You see one needy person, and you minister to them. Then you see another, and you do the same, and before you know it you've ministered to a lot of people."

You may be used to touch many people. But never lose sight of what ministry really is. It is ministering to the one. That's what Jesus did. Whether it was the woman at the well, Zacchaeus or a man called Legion, He took them as divine appointments.

Get Out of Jail!

Paul recognized that he could do nothing of significance in his own strength. Without God, we can't do anything. But with Him, *"I can do all things through Christ who strengthens me."*[12] We may not feel worthy, but it has absolutely nothing to do with us or how we feel! Jesus paid the price. He gave us His power to defeat all of Satan's assaults, including sickness. Through Him, we've been made worthy to receive all of God's good gifts.

The enemy will try to attack your sense of worth, but stand your ground!

The price has been paid in full—for sickness, poverty and death. That means we can expect to have health, prosperity and abundant life. Many people have abused the message of prosperity, but we can't throw the baby out with the bathwater! Jesus wants you to prosper and to be in health. There is nothing wrong with prosperity.

Dick Dewert, a dear friend, launched the first twenty four-hour all-Christian television station in Lethbridge, Alberta. But he had a God-given vision to expand across the entire nation via satellite. To do so, he needed two million dollars. They declared the Word of God over the situation, sowed their financial seed faithfully, and called in an abundant harvest. They fully expected it to become reality.

One day, while he was in Toronto, a man he'd never met approached him and asked to speak to him over coffee. The man said to Dick, "God told me to give you a million dollars." There in the coffee shop, he wrote a cheque for one million dollars! It was the catalyst to launch the Miracle Channel across Canada, declaring the Good News. That is prosperity!

Christ has paid the price for you to be well—physically, emotionally, financially and spiritually. Isaiah 53:4,5 says,

> *"Surely He has borne our griefs And carried our sorrows; Yet we esteemed Him stricken, Smitten by God, and afflicted. But He was wounded for our*

transgressions, He was bruised for our iniquities; The chastisement for our peace was upon Him, And by His stripes we are healed."

That is good news! He has already taken our sicknesses and pains upon Himself, so why should we take them back? Isaiah's words are not hesitant; they state a fact. God wants us to be well. He has paid the price for us to have peace, a peace beyond understanding that comes from the Prince of Peace.

Jesus the Healer and Jesus the Saviour are not two separate entities. Throughout the Gospels, He often spoke of being made "whole."[13] You cannot separate spiritual, emotional and physical wholeness. He paid one price, in full.

We are redeemed. We've been set free. The ransom has been paid.

It's like we were in prison with no way out, but He's come and unlocked the door! We are no longer bound by sin, sickness or poverty. He tells us, "Go—you are free!" But instead of walking out into freedom, we often stay in the prison and say, "Yes, I've heard all about that. But it seems I'm still in jail."

So again He points to the open doors and says, "You are free—go." And again, we don't step out, we fail to listen, and we remain sitting in that jail cell.

So finally, Jesus asks, "Don't you believe that you have been set free? Don't you believe that you have been pardoned? Don't you believe that you can go?"

If you are bound by pain, sickness or disease, this is a message of hope for you: The door is open. Rise up and walk into freedom!

Rise up and send sickness back to hell!

---

[1] Philippians 1:21.

[2] Deuteronomy 34:5-8.

[3] 2 Kings 2:11.

[4] Genesis 5:24.

[5] Deuteronomy 34:7.

[6] Mark 16:18.

[7] Mark 11:23.

[8] Ephesians 2:8.

[9] John 4:1-6.

[10] Luke 19:1-10.

[11] Luke 4:35.

[12] Philippians 4:13.

[13] Mark 5:34; Luke 8:48; 17:19; John 5:6, KJV.

Chapter Three

It's in the Will

Read the Will!

If it's God's will to heal anybody, it's God's will to heal everybody! If it is God's will for you to be sick, then why would you ever consult a doctor? He might just cure you! You should never take medication, because you might get better!

God is not a respecter of persons. He loves everyone equally.

I've looked, but I can't find one verse or passage of Scripture that tells me God wants us to be sick. Instead, I've found countless references to Jesus' suffering for us, taking our pain and sickness on Himself. He bore our sufferings to the cross because He wanted us to be well. God's will for us is that we be healthy and prosper! That means our bodies—not just our souls.[1]

Only once in Scripture do we find someone questioning Jesus about His will. In Mark 1:40, we read of a leper kneeling before Jesus, saying, *"If You are willing, You can make me clean."* How often have you heard believers utter the same words? "Lord, if it's your will to heal me...." Jesus response was, *"I am willing; be cleansed."*[2]

Many times in our healing meetings, when people have received a miracle, I'll ask them, "Did you expect to be healed?" More often than not, they'll respond by saying, "I knew God *could* heal me." Just knowing that God "can" heal is not faith, but knowing that He wants to and *will* heal is.

Suppose for a moment that you marry a billionaire. You live in a large mansion, have a large household staff, a private jet and yacht—everything money could possibly buy. Do you get the picture?

Now, imagine with me that your spouse suddenly passes away. What do you do? Suppose you move out of the mansion, walk away from all the luxury. For months you try to survive on nothing. Finally, in your poverty and desperation, you go to your spouse's lawyer, grovelling, apologizing for bothering him, and explain, "I know my spouse had billions of dollars and that he left you instructions to look after his estate when he was gone. Do you think it would be possible to get just a little bit of his money to buy some food and necessities?"

Is that what you'd do? Of course not! The first thing you'd do is check the will! You'd find out what your inheritance is. And if you find out that your spouse left you his fortune, you would immediately instruct his lawyer to give you all that is rightfully yours!

Or suppose one day, out of the blue, you receive a letter from a lawyer's office, telling you that your rich uncle has passed away and left a million dollars to you in his will. Would you react by saying, "Well, if the lawyer decides I can have the money, it will be wonderful. In the meantime, I'll just get along without it"? No, you wouldn't! It is your rightful inheritance. You would immediately take the necessary steps to collect your inheritance. If the lawyer refused to give it to you, you'd take the will to a judge and tell him, "This is my inheritance; it's in the will."

The Bible is God's will. It is His covenant—His promise to us. Within its pages lies our inheritance. Everything is written down in black and white, leaving no doubt as to what He wants you to have—your inheritance. Are you living in poverty? Are you living with sickness or disease? Perhaps it's time to read the will!

There is only one person to ever write a will, die, and then come back to make sure that it is carried out. That person is Jesus! If you want to know the will of God, read the New Testament, the New Will. If you want to know God's purpose for you, read His will. The four Gospels record Jesus' own words to believers, His promises, and His purpose for them. He came to show us God's heart, and He said several times that He came to do the will of the Father.[3]

Once in a service as I was ministering to people who had come for healing, I overheard someone say, "God would never heal me." I turned and said, "What did you say?" She was embarrassed that I'd heard her, but then she said, "He would never heal me, because I don't deserve it." Right then and there I explained to her, and to the congregation, that it had nothing to do with her goodness. If we all got what we deserved, we'd be in hell! But God, by His grace and mercy, sent Jesus to pay the price for our sickness and sin and to give us peace and provision. He signed His covenant with Christ's blood[4] so that we could, through His righteousness, receive all of the promises in the will.

Jesus is Jesus, Even Today!

"Jesus Christ is the same yesterday, today, and forever."[5] So often, however, we act like Jesus stopped healing people 2000 years ago.

In John 11, we read the account of Jesus' friends, Mary and Martha. Their brother Lazarus was very sick, and they sent word to Jesus to come. But Jesus delayed His coming, obviously to teach them a very important lesson. By the time He arrived, Lazarus had been dead and in the grave for four days. When He saw Martha, Jesus assured her Lazarus would live again, and her response was (paraphrased), "Yes, I believe that 'one day' he'll be alive and well, over in glory, walking on those streets of gold..." She believed in *the Jesus of tomorrow*, *the Jesus of the future*, but couldn't see Him as *the Jesus of today*! In her eyes, a miracle was now impossible.

Mary's cry to Jesus was *"Lord, if You had been here, my brother would not have died."*[6] Now it was too late. Jesus wasn't there while they still had hope; He'd waited too long, and the situation was hopeless. She saw Him as *the Jesus of the past*, but like Martha, didn't understand His power is eternal—He is the same yesterday, today, and forever!

Many believe in *the Jesus of the future*. They think, "Healing is for heaven, where there will be no more pain and sorrow. Jesus will wipe away every tear...someday! In the meantime we'll just have to wait for that day and suffer until Jesus comes."

We pray what He taught us, *"Your kingdom come. Your will be done On earth as it is in heaven."*[7] There is no sickness or pain in heaven, so when we pray for His will on *earth* as it is in *heaven*, we can confidently expect healing. We don't have to wait for heaven—He is King of kings and Lord of lords now, not just in the future! We must believe in the *Jesus of today.*

Most Christians believe in *the Jesus of the past.* They accept the Bible accounts of His miracles and say, "If only I'd been alive when He walked on the shores of Galilee, or on the streets of Jerusalem, healing the sick. If I'd been there, I know I would have been healed."

The truth is that, if the Bible is believable, then Jesus *is* the same yesterday, today and forever. That means that anything He did in the past He is able and willing to do right now!

Not only is He the Jesus of right now, He is the Jesus of right here! What He can do in other places of the world, He can do right here as well. When you hear news of supernatural miracles happening in Africa, Argentina or anywhere else in the world, you have to know that God wants to do the same here, right where you live!

If anyone says, "I believe in healing, *but...*" or "I believe in miracles, *but...*" they're really saying that they don't really believe. You can't qualify faith with a "but." Either you believe God's Word is true, or you don't. It really is very simple. When you pray for healing, you must believe that it is God's will to heal. And you can believe, if you just read His will!

If it is God's will to *save* everyone, it is His will to *heal* everyone. Psalm 103:2-3 says, *"Bless the LORD, O my soul, And forget not all His benefits: Who forgives all your iniquities, Who heals all your diseases."*

I am often asked, after quoting this verse, "If you really believe everyone can be healed, why don't you go to the hospital, heal everyone and empty all the beds?"

My answer is that Jesus Himself didn't do that. He did not heal everyone on earth. In fact, one day He went to the pool of Bethesda, which was crowded with sick people, healed only one man, and left. He did not heal them all.

Sometimes it was because they rejected Him.[8] Sometimes it was because of their wrong motives.[9] But in every instance, those who came to Him expecting, believing, received.[10]

People occasionally come to me and ask if I've ever seen someone healed of a particular disease or ailment. That question troubles me, because it infers that if I've never seen that specific illness healed before, then maybe God won't heal that condition. I understand that when you hear of someone being healed of a condition that you suffer from, it sparks faith. But just because you've never seen a particular condition healed, it doesn't take away from God's ability to do it.

A few years ago we went to Dudley, England, for a healing conference. A young woman was healed of multiple sclerosis on the first night. It was one of those spectacular, instant things. She was a very empty-looking lady who dragged herself in with help, and God touched her in that meeting. She threw down her canes and started to walk and then run. For the first time in years she was absolutely pain-free. All of her muscles and nerves were working, and she was obviously and understandably excited. That night she gave her life to Jesus, and it was an amazing transformation. She left that service absolutely radiating with God's love.

We later learned that she had been in a rehabilitation program because of a drug problem. So, many of her friends were people she had met in that same facility. When she left that night, she went and told them what God had done. The next evening, several of them came to the conference, and God touched, saved, healed and delivered them. By the fourth night it became obvious that we couldn't end the conference. We were just beginning! The fifth night was better than the fourth night, and so on. We ended up staying for seven weeks.

In the course of those exciting meetings, a man was healed of arthritis in his hands. He went home and told his wife he was going to take her mother the next night. His mother-in-law was crippled with arthritis and not a born-again believer. They didn't know if they could even convince her to go. But she did go, and she was healed, and even better, she gave her life to Jesus.

The mother-in-law, in turn, brought her son and his family the following night. One of the grandsons had cerebral palsy, and the other had a skin condition all over his body. I prayed for the entire family in the service. There was no immediate evidence that anything had changed, so they left seemingly unchanged.

Over the course of the next few days, however, the boy with cerebral palsy began to do things that he couldn't do before. The parents took him back to the doctor, and the doctor was astounded. He had never seen cerebral palsy symptoms reversed. The boy with the skin condition was healed, too, and eventually the whole family made a commitment to Christ as a result.

During that time of revival in Dudley, more multiple sclerosis healings took place. We had never seen that before in our ministry. When we came back to Canada, word started to spread that all those healings had taken place, and people with multiple sclerosis began to show up at the meetings.

I was in St. John's, Newfoundland, and a woman came because she had heard that someone in our meetings in England had been healed of multiple sclerosis. She came believing that if God could do it for them, He could do it for her. She was healed, and in the process, our faith level for healing from multiple sclerosis was constantly growing.

There is a reason why certain people see more healings of particular conditions when they pray for people. It's because they've exercised their faith in that area. I understand that, but God is also looking for people to take the Scripture at face value and believe that if God says He heals *all* our diseases, that means *all*. It makes no difference whether I've ever seen it before or not; He heals *all* our diseases!

If...

The Bible contains two types of covenants: *conditional* and *unconditional*.

After Adam and Eve's fall in the Garden of Eden, sin entered the world and placed a wall of separation between God and mankind—the curse I wrote about in the previous chapter. God, however, promised that He would send One (Jesus) who would bruise the head of the serpent (the devil).[11] God kept His promise despite all that had transpired. Galatians 4:4 says, *"But when the fullness of the time had come* [the time when He would fulfill the covenant], *God sent forth His Son."* This covenant, made by God in the Garden, was *unconditional*. Man didn't have to do anything to deserve it or cause it to happen. It was God's plan.

Healing, however, is the result of a *conditional* covenant. If we keep our part of the bargain, God will keep

His! If we treat our bodies as a gift from God, obey the rules—rules of freedom, not rules of bondage—we can fully expect God to keep us in divine health.

God's rules are like train tracks. If a train remains on the tracks, it will reach its destination. If it doesn't—for whatever reason—stay on the track, it will be derailed and destroyed and cause destruction to everything in its path. God desires that we stay "on track" and follow His rules—not to restrict or bind us, but so that we can reach our destination.

In Exodus 15:26, we read about this conditional covenant.

> *"If you diligently heed the voice of the Lord your God and do what is right in His sight, give ear to His commandments and keep all His statutes, I will put none of the diseases on you which I have brought on the Egyptians. For I am the Lord who heals you."*

Based on this covenant, God brought the people of Israel out of Egypt in a "bubble"—the bubble of the blessing of God. As long as they were obedient to Him, they remained in perfect health. I believe that covenant of blessing continues to this day. God is bringing us back into a season of spiritual, physical and emotional blessing.

We live in a day when people break their promises, break their commitments, break their covenants. But *"God is not a man, that He should lie."*[12] If our faith is founded on the Word of God, then we can rest assured that God's promise of healing will be fulfilled.

The reason many believers have trouble accepting divine healing is that they base their faith on what they see, not on God's sure promise.

The covenant in Exodus 15:26 ends with the declaration, *"I am the LORD who heals you."* The form of the verb used here implies a continual healing. "I am the Lord who continually heals you" or "I am the Lord who keeps you healed." It is wonderful to get healed but even more wonderful to stay healed!

You may object, "But I prayed for somebody in faith, and they weren't healed. If healing is a covenant, why didn't it happen?"

There are several possible reasons some aren't healed, some of which I explore in my book, *Six Keys to Breakthrough in Healing*. But there is another reason as well.

This covenant of healing begins with the word *if*. *If* we do not keep our part, God is not obligated to keep His part. *If* we break the covenant, we cannot expect God to keep it either. But often, even after breaking our end of the covenant, when we have not kept our end of the bargain, we expect God to show mercy to us! It is not enough to just *know* the Word of God; we also must "*do what is right in His sight, give ear to His commandments and keep all His statutes.*" Then, God will not allow any diseases to befall us.

Rules? What Rules?

Sabbath

One of the most priceless possessions God has entrusted to us is our human body. And one day we will have to stand before the throne of God and give account for how we have treated this truly amazing gift. There are many believers around the world who are spiritually and physically broken because they have not kept the rules pertaining to their bodies.

Many of us come from a generation that believed "It is better to burn out than to rust out." This belief, however, goes against God's basic rules. What are these rules? One of the rules—a commandment established in God's Word—is the *Sabbath*. Many Christians, especially preachers and Christian leaders, are the greatest Sabbath-breakers, either because they just don't want to waste a moment or because the congregation expects the pastor to serve them seven days a week.

A friend of mine, an evangelist, called me while on vacation a while ago and told me that he was feeling guilty because he was sitting by a lake, resting. My immediate response to him was "Let's pray and break this demonic guilt right now!"

On another occasion, a lady approached me to express her disagreement with my statement about the need for rest and refreshing. "I don't believe that stuff about taking time off," she said. "I've been a Christian for years, and I've never taken a single day off as a holiday. The devil never takes a day off, and I shouldn't either!"

In response, I asked, "Do you want to be like the devil? When did he become our role model?"

Jesus took time off, before or after ministering to people. We see it several times in the Gospels as He asks His disciples to "come away" and rest.[13] They would go away, rest, pray, and return refreshed and ready to meet the opportunities that lay ahead.

For those of us who come from traditional Christian families, the Sabbath, or the day of rest, might take on a particular connotation. For instance, I grew up in a rural setting, in a nominally Christian home, but we kept the rule of Sabbath. On Sundays we would do no activities other than go to church. We weren't allowed to go out and play; nor were we allowed to play inside! We were taught the

Sabbath meant rest. If a farmer went out into his fields on Sunday, other farmers in the area would most certainly show their disapproval and tell him his crops were in trouble because he broke God's law!

At the other end of the spectrum are those to whom a day of rest means nothing. Nowadays most retail stores and restaurants are open on Sunday. Or often, people claim they are just so busy they "can't afford" to rest. For many, their weekday obligations have spilled over into the weekend, and they find themselves busy seven days a week.

I don't know if you have noticed, but computers not only have not eased our workload, they have made our lives even more complicated! We spend much of our waking hours sending or answering e-mails, or typing our own letters that were once the duty of a secretary. Then there are the times when our computer "freezes" or the Internet is "down" and we are held hostage to it until it decides to co-operate (or one of our kids has time to fix it!). Just before the year 2000, we travelled to Russia's Arctic to minister to some of the last nomadic Eskimos in the world. As I was sitting hundreds of miles from nowhere, in the middle of the tundra in a reindeer-skin tent, with those Nenet people at the very ends of the earth, for a moment I envied them. They didn't know anything about Y2K and the predicted disaster of computers crashing all over the world. Their lives would go on exactly as they always had. Power outages, energy crises, global financial collapse—none of those things held any significance for those nomadic reindeer herders.

If we expect to walk in divine health, we must take time off. Our bodies and minds need rest. I admit there are weeks when our schedules do not allow us to take a day of rest. For instance, I may have just returned home from a busy ministry trip and several days of recording television programs, allowing me no time to rest. However, understanding God's rule of the Sabbath, I would schedule a few days off the following week in order to recover and allow my body and mind to rest.

Violating this rule bears heavy consequences. We may get away with it for months, or even years, but it will eventually catch up to us. I know of people right now who have God's call on their lives, but because they have abused their bodies for so long, they can't respond to the call.

It's taken thirty years for me to learn this principle. I have learned that when I am tired, I cannot minister in strength. I've learned that I have to allow time for rejuvenation, for refreshing, for rest. Those days are actually scheduled into my calendar at the beginning of every year, forcing me to take retreat days—to do nothing else but rest.

What Goes in...

Another rule is that we should not abuse our bodies by taking in things that are unhealthy. Smoking, for instance, may not keep us from going to heaven (in fact, it might get you there quicker!), but it will have devastating effects on our health.

If God miraculously heals you of a lung condition caused by smoking, but you continue to smoke, your "new" set of lungs will not be exempt from the adverse effects of nicotine. God, in His mercy, does sometimes heal us even when we don't keep our end of the covenant, but that's not what I'm talking about. I'm talking about living and walking in consistent, absolute health.

Eating properly ties into this same principle. I used to think that in order to be a good steward, I had to stay in the cheapest places and eat the cheapest food. I found out the hard way that, in fact, I was being a poor steward of my health. I was abusing my body.

In the very early years of my travelling ministry, I developed gout as a result of my poor eating habits. When the doctor found out that my diet consisted almost entirely of fast food, he put me on diet of fresh fruits and vegetables for one month. Before long I was in good health again, and I'd learned a hard lesson. Poor eating habits will take a toll on your health.

At the time of preparing this book, I am about to turn sixty, and I feel great! Some of the young people on our staff find it difficult to keep up with my wife and I and our schedule. We owe our vitality to God's goodness and doing our best to monitor "what goes in."

A few years ago, some of my friends were telling me that, at my age, I should have regular physical checkups. I realized I didn't even have a doctor. So I decided to ask a friend who is doctor if he would be willing to give me a checkup. He agreed, so I booked an appointment. I had X-rays, blood work, heart tests and the usual examinations.

A few days later, the doctor called me and said, "Bill, we got the test results. My goodness! You're a healthy man! I'd be hard pressed to find a sixteen-year-old with such good results. Your heart, blood pressure and cholesterol levels are absolutely amazing!" The next time I saw him, he asked me to pray for him because he wanted to be as healthy as I am!

You keep your word; I'll keep mine

Some of us think that the more we do for God, the more He'll like us. We may not verbalize this mentality, but we do think it and act accordingly. We feel we have to prove our worth to God, but that couldn't be further from the truth. We don't have to prove anything to Him.

God often heals unbelievers. It seems rather odd to us that there are people who have been in the church for years, waiting and praying for healing, when suddenly some ungodly person walks in one day and receives a miracle.

I remember once, during a service in Toronto, God gave me a word of knowledge about a healing. Immediately, a young man came forward. I prayed for him, and he received a miraculous healing. Later on, I gave an altar call for salvation, and this young man was the first to come forward. I asked him, "Are you rededicating your life to Christ?" He answered, "No, this is the first time I've ever been in a church!"

I had assumed that he had received healing because he had great faith. But the fact is, he had no faith at all. God showed him His love by healing him, and, as a result, this man gave his life to Jesus.

It is important to understand that God heals unbelievers, not because of their worth or their faith, but out of His mercy. It is His way of saying, "I love you, and I want to demonstrate my love to you." When Philip went to Samaria, they received the message of salvation because of the miracles.[14]

Believers, on the other hand, are dealt with on a different principle. God made a covenant with His people—a conditional covenant. He is not obligated to fulfill His part of the covenant if we do not fulfill ours.

Even revival, according to Scripture, is a conditional covenant. In 2 Chronicles 7:14 we read,

> *"If My people who are called by My name will humble themselves, and pray and seek My face, and*

turn from their wicked ways, then I will hear from heaven, and will forgive their sin and heal their land."

Healing of the land is revival. God said He would bring about healing *if* His people did certain things. Revival and healing of the land are related and dependent on believers—"*My people*"—not the ungodly. The conditions people must keep are to humble themselves, pray, seek God's face and turn from their wicked ways. As much as I respect and appreciate those who fast and pray for revival in their nations, I must emphasize that revival only comes when Christians approach God's altar in humility of heart, confess their sins and set their lives right with God.

If you study the life of Samson, you'll see that he broke the law, defiled himself, lowered his standards and compromised—and still God's blessing was on him. It was in cutting his hair that the anointing of God left him. Cutting his hair in itself was not important; God doesn't get "hung up" over the length of our hair or the kind of clothes we wear. But Samson had made a covenant with God concerning his hair, and he broke it. Breaking the covenant was a very serious act, for which God held Samson accountable.

As believers, unless we fulfill our obligations in the covenant, God is in no way obligated to heal us. Out of His goodness, He does at times heal us despite our failure to keep our end of the covenant. But if we want to live consistently in health, we must fulfill our part of the covenant. When we do, this covenant ensures that God, because He has given His word to do His part, will keep His promise and heal us!

But Daddy, You Promised!

My wife and I have had the privilege of raising four children—two girls and two boys. They are all grown up now with families of their own. When they were little, they would come to me and ask for things. They would ask boldly, without hesitation, because they knew I loved them.

It was fascinating to see their differing personalities emerge. Each of them used unique tactics if they wanted something they were not sure they could get. They knew some "manipulation" would be necessary!

Our oldest daughter, Margie, learned at a very early age that she could get just about anything from me by using her big, beautiful eyes. All she had to do was sit on my knee, look at me with those big eyes and plead, "Daddy, pleeease." I would melt! Even now, she knows how to get what she wants from me!

Our youngest son, Steve, is a negotiator. He learned the skills of negotiation at a very early age. He would come go to my wife an hour before lunchtime and ask, "Mommy, can I have six cookies?" Gwen would answer, "Absolutely not! It's almost lunch time."

So he would say, "Can I have five cookies?" Again she would say, "No." He'd continuing asking, lowering the number, until he got some. He almost always was given two cookies! He knew that if he started by asking for one cookie and the answer was "no," he'd have nothing to negotiate with. Interestingly enough, in the process, he made his mother feel like she had won the argument!

There were times that the answer to my children's request was an immediate "yes." Other times, it was "no" or "not yet." For example, if my son when he was nine years old had asked if he could drive the car to school, the answer would have been a definite "no!"

Some people who go to God about healing take these types of approaches. They beg, manipulate or negotiate with God. Or they don't know if they'll receive, because they think He may say "no" or "not yet." They don't understand the covenant.

Healing is not something that needs to be negotiated with God. He has promised healing, and He will keep His word. We do not need to beg for healing or speculate whether or not it's God's will to heal us. It is His promise.

In my earlier years of ministry, while our children were still quite young, I'd be preparing to go away on a ministry trip and one of them might say, "Daddy, we don't want you to go." I would give them a big hug and assure them, "I have to go to tell people about Jesus. But when I come back, we'll do something special together." Unfortunately, they wouldn't let me off the hook that easily. We had to decide exactly what were going to do upon my return.

Usually something as simple as the promise of a trip to McDonald's or a trip to an ice cream shop would satisfy them. The moment I was back at home, weary and thinking only of having a rest, the children would come running into my arms and remind me, "Daddy, you said we'd go to McDonald's. You promised!" And of course I'd be obligated to do what I'd promised.

The *promise* was their assurance that their father would keep his word.

That is exactly how it is with our heavenly Father. You can come to Him and say, "Father, you promised!" Since He is a God who keeps His word, He will do exactly what He has promised. You can count on it!

---

[1] 3 John 2.

[2] Mark 1:41.

[3] Luke 22:42; John 4:34; 5:30.

[4] 1 Corinthians 11:24-30.

[5] Hebrews 13:8.

[6] John 11:32.

[7] Matthew 6:10.

[8] Mark 6:5-6.

[9] Mark 8:11,12.

[10] Matthew 4:24.

[11] Genesis 3:14-15.

[12] Numbers 23:19.

[13] Mark 6:31.

[14] Acts 8:6.

Chapter Four

Get Ready to Be Healed

Take Your Time

Taking time to prepare before doing battle with the enemy is so important that I feel it needs to be addressed in this chapter.

Although I personally felt a great sense of urgency after being called to the ministry, I had to spend several years going through Bible college training, getting practical experience, and developing my spiritual life to prepare me for what God had in store. And that was just the beginning! Every day, I discover fresh truths and revelations of the Spirit.

As a young boy, David was anointed to be king of Israel. Yet, he still had to tend his father's sheep for several years before he faced the giant Goliath. But when he did, he was ready! Saul and the army of Israel had studied the enemy;

they had become experts on giants—giantologists! They spent every waking hour listening to the giant's taunts, and even when Goliath happened to be quiet, they would think about him. They were intimidated by his size, by his strength and by his massive armour.

That's why Saul asked David for his qualifications when he volunteered to face this ruthless enemy. Had he killed giants before? Did he know anything about giants? What kind of weapon was he going to use?

Listen to David's reply:

> *"Your servant used to keep his father's sheep, and when a lion or a bear came and took a lamb out of the flock, I went out after it and struck it, and delivered the lamb from its mouth; and when it arose against me, I caught it by its beard, and struck and killed it."*[11]

When he faced a ferocious bear, David put his faith into action—no one watching—just him and the bear. David knew that this creature was bigger than he was, but he also knew that God was bigger than the beast!

His faith had grown over time. First he faced the bear, then the lion, and now he stood in front of the Philistine giant. He had experienced God's hand of deliverance before, and he knew what the outcome would be this time.

> *"Your servant has killed both lion and bear; and this uncircumcised Philistine will be like one of them, seeing he has defied the armies of the living God." Moreover David said, "The Lord, who delivered me from the paw of the lion and from the paw of the bear, He will deliver me from the hand of this Philistine."*[12]

Instead of focusing in on how big the giant was, David decided to tell the giant how big his God was!

In the same way, as believers, our faith will not increase by studying every detail about a problem or a sickness. Often, in praying for a condition or circumstance, we tell God how big the problem is. But, like David, all we really need to do is tell the problem how powerful God is!

Cute Little Cubs

There are certain things, however, that might hinder God's anointing on our lives. During our times of preparation, it is absolutely necessary that we identify these hindrances, face up to them and allow God to remove them.

Have you ever seen a lion cub up close? They are so cute and cuddly! But how often have you heard stories about people taking in a cute little cub and raising it as a pet? Years later, when the cub has grown into an adult lion, it turns against its owners, mauls them, and sometimes even kills them.

A similar scenario was played out in the news recently as Roy Horn (of Siegfried & Roy, Las Vegas entertainers known for their act featuring the use of tigers), narrowly escaped death as one of his "pet" tigers grabbed him by the throat and dragged him offstage. He has undergone months of painful recovery and reconstructive surgery. We can so easily be deceived by the small and seemingly innocent things that come into our lives.

There is something in all of us that makes us think we are different, that we'll be able to handle seemingly "harmless" habits and vices, just like cute little cubs. The sad truth is that often the thing we thought we could control soon controls us. The destructive results are always heartbreaking.

Every year, people from all over the world travel to Churchill, Manitoba, the "polar bear capital of the world," in hopes of seeing polar bears up close. They truly are a beautiful animal and an amazing sight to see.

In order to get close, tourists are taken out on the land in a cage-like vehicle to the bears' natural habitat. But before the expedition begins, the driver takes time to warn his passengers about the danger of trying to touch the bears through the bars of the cage. I have heard many stories about polar bears from my Inuit friends. Although these animals look cute and innocent, they can be deadly, easily taking someone's head off with one swipe of a paw. And on these outings, inevitably somebody ignores the driver's warnings, for the sake of the "thrill of danger." It's a risky game to play.

That's a picture of some believers. They test God's grace, seeing how close they can get to activities and temptations that on the surface seem harmless enough. Sooner or later they will learn a hard lesson: you can't play with lions and bears—even if they're cubs—and avoid getting hurt. Eventually that little cub will grow into a beast!

I was asked to speak on the topic of sexual addiction at a Christian men's retreat a few years ago. At first I was reluctant. I was sure the subject matter wouldn't apply to these men. Almost all of them were Spirit-filled, active believers. However, I agreed and prepared accordingly because the organizers felt impressed by the Spirit that this was the direction I should go in.

I spoke as openly and honestly as I could, addressing the pitfalls and the biblical basis for keeping a pure heart. At the end of the session, I would have been much more comfortable just giving a general prayer, but I sensed the Lord directing me to ask if there was anyone struggling with this problem and needing prayer. I assured them that everyone in the room would not judge them but would join me in believing for their deliverance.

To my utter amazement, all but a few in the entire crowd came forward and confessed that this was a real problem for them. For many of them, their addiction had begun by viewing Internet sites. Before long they found themselves helplessly addicted to pornography.

Others had even more serious sexual addictions that started with what they thought was harmless experimentation. But soon their occasional "indiscretions" had spiralled out of control. Until that moment, neither the group's leaders or myself realized what a serious and widespread problem this was.

The following year, I was invited back to conduct a similar session at the same retreat. Again, at the end of the meeting, almost everyone came forward—and several of them were the same men who had responded the previous year! I couldn't understand why, at first.

They had asked Jesus to break the chains of bondage in their lives. And they had the assurance that, *"If the Son sets you **free**, you will **indeed be free**."*[3] But they also needed to make a serious commitment to become accountable and to keep their minds continually renewed.[4]

Sooner or later, there comes a time when you have to get serious about staying away from sin. You can't continue to entertain the same thoughts and temptations that bound you in the first place. These "bears and lions" must be defeated, once and for all.

The blood of Jesus cleanses us, but once we are clean we must continually stay clean. A farmer can clean his pig up, but as long as the mud hole remains inside the pen, you can be sure the pig will return to it! It's the same with us.

We need to take every necessary step to ensure the bears and lions in our lives are really "dead." Fill your mind with the Word of God, listen to uplifting messages and music, and cultivate your relationship with the Lord. Surround yourself with strong, supportive people of God who will hold you accountable and help you when you feel weak.

Take practical steps to remove every temptation from your life. If it is pornography, get software to block offending Web sites and keep your computer in a location visible to others. If your addiction is to drugs, alcohol or another habit-forming substance, stay away from places where it is accessible and refuse to have it in your home.

When the Spirit of God reveals bears and lions in your life and you refuse to deal with them, how then can you expect to slay the giants? You'll thwart God's purpose and plans for you to fulfill your ministry and destiny—and it won't be His fault! He wants to work through clean vessels.

Ham, or Turkey?

If we desire a successful and consistent healing ministry, we must be filled with the Word of God, claim it and stand on its promises. Jesus tells us, *"If you abide in Me, and My words abide in you, you will ask what you desire, and it shall be done for you."*[5]

Christians are in no way exempt from the attacks of the enemy. Even Jesus Himself had to overcome the enemy's attacks in the wilderness! However, every time the devil opened his mouth, Jesus responded by quoting Scripture, saying, *"It is written..."*[6]

Our greatest weapon to defeat the enemy is the Word of God—not our emotions or intellect. That's the reason the enemy tries to prevent believers from remaining in God's Word—he is all too well aware of its power. The more the Word is in us, the more God is in us.

Abraham, for instance, was so filled with the promises of God that he became unreasonable. He hoped "*against hope*." When his circumstances told him that fathering a child was impossible, he refused to believe them—instead he believed God's promise.[7] And he received the promise!

In Psalm 107:20 we read, *"He sent His word and healed them."* The power of God for healing is in His Word. Ministries that are blessed by God are "Word-based" ministries. Overcoming Christians are "Word-based" Christians. In the face of sickness, we must declare the Word of God!

We, as believers, can be distracted very easily. How often do we find ourselves focusing on things that really aren't important? Can you believe that churches have split over such petty things as the colour of the carpet or the choice of songs! Some pastors spend much of their time contending with and appeasing people upset over such trivial little things, day in and day out. It's time to get focused on the essentials again!

Even when Jesus Christ was here on earth, he was continually bombarded with trivial disputes. A group of religious leaders, Sadducees, came to Him and said, *"Moses said that if a man dies, having no children, his brother shall marry his wife and raise up offspring for his brother."* They continued by presenting a hypothetical situation where, based on this law of Moses, a widow was passed along to seven brothers, following the deaths of one brother after another. The question they posed was, *"In the resurrection, whose wife of the seven will she be?"*[8]

When we read this scenario, we usually pass over the significance of this Mosaic law. But imagine if that were still the practice today! Suppose you have a married brother who dies, making his wife a widow. The executor of the will calls you and says, "Congratulations, you've just inherited your sister-in-law!" (I can almost hear some of you groaning, as you put faces and names on your personal scenario!)

Jesus didn't allow the Sadducees to distract him. Their question concerning the resurrection was pointless—they didn't even believe in the resurrection. They just wanted to trap Jesus. They wanted to distract Him from His main purpose.

I remember as a young man in Bible college, hearing rather heated discussions about such unimportant things, such as "Did Adam have a belly button?" or hypothetical questions, such as "Could God make a boulder so heavy even He couldn't lift it?"! These are useless distractions, just like the Sadducees' question regarding the resurrection.

One time, years ago, shortly after we began pastoring a tiny church in a small town, my wife Gwen was asked to speak at a ladies' meeting. As a means for outreach, all the ladies of the church had been encouraged to bring a friend. So, filled with great anticipation, Gwen left for the meeting.

She returned home that night very disturbed. As it turned out, the ladies had indeed brought friends, and there was a rather large crowd gathered. Just before turning the meeting over to my wife, the leaders explained that they needed the church ladies to make some decisions regarding a regional function they'd be hosting.

The main question on the agenda was whether to serve ham or turkey. The discussion apparently got so heated that it almost came to blows as those Christian ladies squabbled over the choice of meats! My wife, as well as all the unsaved ladies, watched the spectacle in horror. The enemy managed to distract this group of ladies from their main purpose by using such a petty matter as turkey or ham!

There really are more important issues at stake. I have to wonder how we'd react today if Jesus showed up to one of our annual church business meetings. What would our response to Him be?

Jesus identified the real issue in His answer to the religious leaders' question regarding the resurrection. He told them, "*You are mistaken, not knowing the Scriptures nor the power of God.*"[9] He then went on to explain the true meaning of the Scripture, and He rebuked them for focusing on the God of the "dead" rather than the "living." In essence, Jesus was telling them that, by studying and debating such Scriptures, they were missing the essentials. They desperately needed balance.

Nowadays, a lot of Christians have a distorted concept of the word *balance*. Believers can usually be identified as in two categories.

The first is made up of dedicated students of the Bible, with a good theological foundation. They certainly know the truth, but they don't have much "life." They are sometimes critical of people whose passion is experiencing God. In their minds, *balance* means abandoning "all that emotional stuff" and focusing on thorough biblical knowledge.

The next group is made up of people who prefer to "feel" and experience God rather than study His Word. They love going to meetings where they see and experience miracles, signs, wonders and the moving of God's Spirit. They feel that those who spend all their time studying the Scriptures are missing the joy and reality of dynamic spiritual life.

The first group accuses the latter of shallowness, while the latter accuses the former of dryness. But Jesus points out that one is not more important than the other—we need to pursue *both* the Scriptures *and* the power of God. We must have a solid knowledge and understanding of the Scriptures *and* the presence and anointing of God's Spirit living in and through us. That is true balance.

The Bible is not just dry, lifeless words of history or philosophy. The Bible is Life—the very essence of God and His power. The psalmist David recognized its value when he said, in Psalm 119:11, *"Your word I have hidden in my heart, That I might not sin against You."*

I once met a lady who was very excited about "experiencing" God. She was so focused on what she wanted to "feel" that she'd become involved in some questionable activities that didn't line up with the Bible. When I tried to caution her by showing her Scripture that conflicted with her experiences, she actually pushed the Bible away and said, "Don't confuse me with Scripture. I don't have time to waste studying the Bible. I'm just so excited about Jesus!"

That response is a total contradiction of who Jesus is! John chapter 1 reveals Him as *the Word*, in fleshly form. If you get excited about Jesus, you get excited about His Word. To love Jesus means loving His Word! The way to know Him better is to know His Word.

We have to allow the truth of the Word to penetrate our hearts and spirits. The Bible is exactly like its Author—

eternal, relevant, and illuminating. It shows us the heart, mind and will of God. When I want to know Jesus more, I go to His Word. When I want to be closer to Him, I go to His Word. When I need healing, I go to His Word.

Imagine this: Jesus calls you on the telephone today and says that He wants to come for a visit. I can't imagine that you'd say, "Well, today isn't really convenient," or, "You'll have to wait until my favourite television program is over." Of course not. You would drop everything and make preparations to spend time with Him.

Jesus *is* the Word made flesh, so we must treat the Bible the same way we'd treat Jesus if He were here in the flesh. Make your time with the Word a priority. If you do, I can honestly guarantee you that it will change your life!

A lot of people say they want God to speak to them. They expect to hear an audible voice or see a vision. Although He does occasionally reveal Himself to us through these supernatural methods, the most reliable and consistent way to hear what He is saying is through His Word. It will give us life and hope, direction and answers to our questions. It will prepare us to receive healing for our body and take this healing anointing to others as well.

Along with developing a strong biblical foundation for your faith, the power of His Word should be evident through you. Healing anointing, the gifts and fruit of the Spirit should be active and obvious in your daily life.

John the Baptist sent his disciples to Jesus with this question, *"Are you really the Messiah we've been waiting for, or should we keep looking for someone else?"*[10] Jesus didn't go into a deep theological explanation, and he didn't begin to rehearse all the prophetic Scriptures that He was and had fulfilled. He simply responded,

> *"Go back to John and tell him about what you have heard [the Word] and seen [the power of God—the blind see, the lame walk, the lepers are cured, the deaf hear, the dead are raised to life, and the Good News is being preached to the poor."*[11]

In other words, Jesus was saying, "The miracles and the Word I preach are proof of Who I am."

Seeing Is Believing? No Way!

When the Word of God is deeply imbedded into your spirit, there won't be any room left for doubts and negative reports. Symptoms of sickness or pain can be huge giants in our lives. I understand that. I also understand how easy it is to allow the symptoms to distract and overwhelm us. Like the army of Israel who faced the giant Goliath, we find ourselves studying the giants.

That is one of the enemy's tactics! He gets us to take our eyes off Jesus, His promises for our health and healing, and to focus on the problem. Before long, we're so overwhelmed by the problem we find it hard to believe for a miracle.

It's our choice. We can decide whether we want to believe Satan—the father of lies—or God's Word, the Truth.

The saying goes, "Seeing is believing." But in our case, as Christians, "Believing is seeing!" Remember Thomas? When Jesus first appeared to the disciples after His resurrection, Thomas wasn't there. When the others told him about it later, he couldn't accept their report because he hadn't see it for himself. He said, *"I won't believe it unless I see the nail wounds in his hands, put my fingers into them, and place my hand into the wound in his side."*[12]

Eight days later Jesus appeared to them again, and this time Thomas was with them and saw Him for himself. Jesus provided every possible proof to Thomas, inviting him to touch the wounds and see the marks on His body. Once Thomas saw for himself, he believed.

Even though we often criticize Thomas for his lack of faith, many of us are just like him. We forget that the world we live in is temporal. We think this is reality. Jesus said to Thomas, *"Because you have seen me, you have believed. Blessed are those who have not seen and yet have believed."*[13]

Even when the evidence, what you see and hear, contradicts God's Word—believe God's Word. That sounds unreasonable, I know, but remember that God is looking for people who are totally unreasonable!

Hebrews 11:1 defines faith: *"Now faith is the substance of things hoped for, the evidence of things not seen."* We don't need faith to believe something tangible—we can see it. Faith brings things that are unseen into being and makes things that are not felt real. God is pleased when we choose to look to His Word only, rather than to the circumstances, to base our faith on His promises instead of the impossibilities. Verse 2 says, *"By it* [faith] *the elders obtained a good testimony."*

Hearing the Word of God produces faith. Our five senses connect to our brain. It tells us to see, hear, smell, feel and taste. But faith goes beyond our natural senses. It must sometimes ignore the senses and trust the "impossibility" of God's ability. *"We walk by faith, not by sight."*[13]

Jesus wasn't dominated by His senses. It was the other way around. His senses were His servants. One time, for instance, He healed a leper by saying "*be cleansed.*" All His natural senses screamed, "He's not cleansed! Look at his twisted limbs, touch his decayed body, smell his rotting flesh, hear his cries of despair, and feel his agony!" But Jesus ignored the symptoms and His natural senses. God's ability wasn't subject to the human senses, and as Jesus spoke the words, the leper was healed.[14]

In Mark 11:14, we read that Jesus cursed a fig tree. At that moment it appeared that nothing happened. The tree didn't fall down or shrivel up, and lightning didn't strike. There was no physical manifestation of the words He spoke. Some of the disciples probably even doubted that anything would happen. But the next day, when they returned, the tree was dead.

Just because we don't see the immediate evidence doesn't mean that nothing has happened. It's a real challenge sometimes to stand in faith, but it's always safe to believe God. Regardless of what our senses tell us, we can trust God.

Abraham is a good example of a person who chose to trust and believe God rather than what his senses told him. Romans 4:18-21 tells us that Abraham,

> *Contrary to hope, in hope believed, so that he became the father of many nations, according to what was spoken, "So shall your descendants be." And not being weak in faith, he did not consider his own body, already dead (since he was about a hundred years old), and the deadness of Sarah's womb. He did not waver at the promise of God through unbelief, but was strengthened in faith, giving glory to God, and being fully convinced that what He had promised, He was also able to perform."*

Abraham hoped against hope. Even though it seemed too late for him and Sarah to have a child, he chose to believe the report of the Lord.

Very often God waits until it is hopeless (at least, what we consider to be hopeless). We'll cry out, "If you don't do it now, it will be too late!" But God doesn't always do *what* we think He should *when* we think He should.

Abraham and Sarah accepted the fact that they would never have a child, because physically it was impossible. It was then—when it was "too late"—that the heavenly messengers came to them with the promise of a child.

Abraham and Sarah's immediate reaction was "It can't be. We are too old." The difference between them and the messengers was that the messengers had just come from the throne room of God. They didn't see the natural and physical state of Abraham and Sarah. They saw the greatness of God!

We, as believers, often find ourselves in the same situation. We've given up on any hope of a miracle and given in to our senses, and God sends a message of hope!

We "know" that nothing is too hard for God, but we must be able to let the truth of His promises penetrate our spirit and move our faith. Abraham ignored his physical senses completely and instead chose to believe God. Sarah *"judged Him faithful who had promised."*[15]

That is faith—hope against hope. Faith knows that God cannot lie. Despite what we see, hear, smell, feel or hear, we cannot allow faith to be moved. Faith loves a challenge, because it knows that *"with God all things are possible"*![16]

Don't let your mountain overwhelm you. Stand back and get proper perspective. Then speak to it, based on God's promise and His power in you, and declare, "Sickness, go to hell!"

---

[1] 1 Samuel 17:34-36.

[2] 1 Samuel 17:36-37.

[3] John 8:36, NLT, emphasis added.

[4] Romans 12:2.

[5] John 15:7.

[6] Matthew 4:4-10.

[7] Romans 4:16-22, KJV.

[8] Matthew 22:24-28.

[9] Matthew 22:29.

[10] Matthew 11:3, NLT.

[11] Matthew 11:4,5, NLT.

[12] John 20:25, NLT.

[13] John 20:29.

[13] 2 Corinthians 5:7.

[14] Luke 5:12,13.

[15] Hebrews 11:11.

[16] Matthew 19:26.

Chapter Five

The Prayer of Faith

Keep On Asking!

Praying in faith simply means to ask God to do what He has already promised to do in His Word. If we fill our hearts and minds with the Word of God, then we know His promises and can stand on them.

Nowhere in the Bible can you find God saying that He wants us to suffer. On the contrary, Isaiah 53:4-6 says He suffered *for us*, carrying our pain and sickness. When you command sickness to "go," you don't have to ask Jesus to take it. He already took it!

That's why I am so confident when I encourage you to tell sickness to "go to hell." Colossians 2:15 tells us that, "*God disarmed the evil rulers and authorities. He shamed them publicly by his victory over them on the cross of Christ*" (NLT).

Revelation 1:18 reminds us that Jesus took the keys to death and hell through His death and resurrection. He took them out of Satan's grasp, so that the enemy can no longer hold us hostage to sin or sickness. Jesus is in charge, and He promises abundant, healthy life!

All the tactics and schemes of the enemy, designed for our destruction, were rendered powerless. It's time for us to remind Satan that he is defeated, and take back what belongs to us!

Many believers think that if they pray the prayer of faith, they'll see immediate results. When the answer isn't instantaneous, they assume that either God has not heard them or the answer just isn't coming. Having this type of mindset, without a proper understanding of the whole Word of God, will sap the life out of our prayers.

The greatest test for any believer in Christ is having *to wait* after praying a prayer of faith. Waiting! Now, personally this is a tough one, as I am impatient by nature. I am the type of person who keeps pressing the elevator button until it arrives.

I don't like stop signs and red lights, because they mean I have to wait, even if there's no traffic coming. I love travelling in England, where they have roundabouts instead. Gwen usually acts as navigator while I drive. When we get on a roundabout, it sometimes takes circling a few times until she finds on the map which road to take. I don't mind that a bit—at least I can keep moving, even if I'm not going anywhere!

I wonder if God sometimes delays the answer to our prayers just to see if we really believe. Between the time God promised a son to Abraham and the actual birth of that son, there was a long period of waiting. But Abraham had faith. He didn't necessarily ignore the facts, but he didn't let them affect his expectation. He decided to move into the realm of faith. He believed in hope when there was no hope![1]

Just like Abraham, we can't try and figure out *how* God is going to do something. If we try to, we'll only confuse and frustrate ourselves and eventually discourage ourselves to the point of giving up. We just have to believe He *will* do what He's promised.

God has His ways—and we simply don't have the capacity to figure it out. Isaiah 55:9 tells us, *"Just as the heavens are higher than the earth, so are my ways higher than your ways..."*(NLT). One thing we *do* know: His ways are always better! In fact, the apostle Paul said He "is able to do ***exceeding abundantly above*** *all that we ask or think..."*[2]

Let's not limit Him to our way of thinking. He'll answer, even if we don't know how or when. We simply can't box Him in like that. That's not how God operates. The key lies simply in what Jesus said, *"Ask, and it will be given to you; seek, and you will find; knock, and it will be opened to you."*[3]

It sounds easy enough, doesn't it? But many Christians become frustrated when they ask and don't seem to receive, when they seek and haven't yet found, when they knock and are still waiting for the door to open.

A few years ago, a believing woman came to me and told me about her son. He was hopelessly addicted to drugs, had left home and was living on the streets. His mother was devastated and feared that at any minute someone might bring her the news of her son's death. I suggested to her that we pray and was shocked when she refused my offer.

She told me she had prayed already and left it with God. If she prayed again, God would think she didn't have faith!

What this woman failed to realize is that persistence is actually a sign of faith. By "leaving it with God," she was actually saying, "It's God's fault if my son doesn't get his life straightened out. I've done my part."

When Jesus told the story, recorded in Luke 18, of the woman and the unjust judge, He was teaching about persistent prayer. In spite of his refusal to give her what she'd requested, the woman kept knocking on the judge's door until finally she got her answer. In other words, Jesus was telling us that if it's worth asking for, then it's worth continuing to ask until you receive. Find someone who will agree in prayer with you—and ask again. Every chance you get, ask!

Jesus told another story, recorded in Luke 15, of a woman who lost a very valuable coin. She didn't just resign herself to the fact that the coin was lost and say, "Oh well; it's gone." On the contrary, she searched everywhere. She swept every corner of her house. She didn't stop until she found what was lost. Seek, and you will find! It's called *persistence*.

A young man who very much wanted to know the Lord more intimately felt he wasn't getting anywhere in his pursuit. He went to talk to an older man who lived by the ocean, because he knew the man had a deep relationship with God.

While they were walking along the shore, the older man started leading the young man out into the water, farther and farther, until the water was at about chest level.

Suddenly, the old man pushed him under water and held him there! The young man instinctively began struggling, thrashing about, fearing for his life. Finally, the old man released him. Gasping and coughing, the young man yelled, "Why did you do that?"

The old man answered, "Until you are as desperate to know God as you were for air when I was holding you under water, you will never really know Him."

How passionately do you want what you're praying for? How badly do you want to receive? The secret of success for many people, whether in business or in spiritual matters, is not found in their talents or abilities. It's in a little thing called *persistence*. They refuse to give up. The reason why so many Christians never achieve their destiny is that as soon as the going gets tough, they quit.

Exercise!

A few years ago, I met a young lady at one of our healing ministry meetings. Her name was Jane. She was a drug user and dealer. Her life was a complete mess. She had cancer and had attempted suicide on several occasions. Coming into the service, she felt so unworthy that she didn't even sit down with the rest of the people there but stood at the back of the hall.

During the service, God gave me a word, saying that someone was being healed of cancer. No one responded. I repeated the word several times until finally this young lady, standing at the back, put her hand on her neck. The lumps that had been there had disappeared! Her cancer was gone!

She began to cry and repeat over and over, "I found it. I found it." When someone asked her what it was that she had found, she replied, "I found love!" That night, she gave her life to Christ. Soon afterward, Jane brought a group of men along with her. These men were "her guys," in charge of collecting money for the drugs she sold.

They were all large, muscle-bound men! That night, every one of them accepted Christ too. From then on, they would come to our meetings and sit right at the front, each one with a big Bible on their laps. They were so eager to learn about God.

After one of the services, I caught my wife staring at the muscular arms of one of these massive men. I told her jokingly, "Honey, he doesn't have anything that I don't!"

And my wife replied, "So what happened to you?"

I thought about that humiliating experience and realized that man and I were born with the exact same muscles. We both have biceps, pectorals, and abs. The difference is that he made a decision and dedicated a good part of his life to working out, developing those muscles. I, on the other hand, haven't!

Faith must be exercised too. Start where you are. Believe God for the small things, and expect Him to answer. Over time, as you see God's faithfulness to deliver on His promises in your life, big things will seem small. *"Is anything too hard for the LORD?"*[4]

I recall very clearly what happened when I first launched into healing ministry. A lady came to me and asked me to pray for her arthritis to be healed. I knew there was no "cure" for arthritis. What she wanted was impossible. I really didn't have much faith, but I obeyed God, laid hands on her and prayed. To my surprise, she was healed! She was totally and completely free from pain, swelling and limitation.

The next day, someone else asked me to pray for healing from arthritis. This time, I was able to pray with more faith because I had already witnessed the healing the night before. Again, the arthritis symptoms completely left. The following night during the service, I took the initiative and asked anyone in the congregation suffering from arthritis to come forward and receive healing! My faith had been developing and strengthened through the previous experiences. I was exercising my faith.

If you decide to begin an exercise program and head off to a gym for the first time, chances are you won't be able to lift your body weight over your head. Instead, you have to start with lighter weights, build your muscles and work your way up.

When my sons were teenagers, they lifted weights regularly. One day, seeing them exercising with their friends, I decided to show off and said, "I can do anything you guys can." They called my bluff and challenged me to lift the same weight they were lifting.

Ignoring my wife's pleas to me against the challenge, I decided to prove my manhood and accepted. They set the weights on the bar and told me to go ahead. It occurred to me this might be a set-up—that they'd put far more weights on than even they could lift—so I said, "You go first." They did—first one, then the other.

Once I knew this test was legitimate, I was confident that, if they could do it, so could I. I lay on the bench, took a deep breath and lifted the barbell off the supports. The moment I did, however, it came right back down, landing on my chest. Gasping for air, I had to beg my sons (who were standing there laughing at me) to help me lift it off. It was a humiliating lesson.

The same thing can happen in ministry. People try to imitate others, starting at someone else's level of faith, and when they fail they are humiliated. You have to start where you are and let your faith grow as you continue to exercise it.

That is how faith is built. Romans 12:3 says, "*God has dealt to each one a measure of faith.*" What we do with the measure we have is completely up to us.

You Do the Obeying; God Will Take Care of the Healing

James 5:13-16 says,

"Is anyone among you suffering? Let him pray. Is anyone cheerful? Let him sing psalms. Is anyone among you sick? Let him call for the elders of the church, and let them pray over him, anointing him with oil in the name of the Lord. And the prayer of faith will save the sick, and the Lord will raise him up. And if he has committed sins, he will be forgiven. Confess your trespasses to one another, and pray for one another, that you may be healed. The effective, fervent prayer of a righteous man avails much."

We are not responsible for the results, but we are responsible to obey. As long as we do our part and obey God, He will do His part and bring healing. James uses the word *anyone*. You and I are both part of that *anyone*.

I wrote at the beginning of this book that if it is God's will to heal *anyone*, then it is God's will to heal *everyone*. I believe that. God's promise is all-inclusive, not selective. The prayer of faith doesn't wonder whether or not God is *willing* to heal; instead, it knows that God *promises* to heal.

The Scriptures say, *"Faith comes by hearing, and hearing by the word of God."*[5] You can't receive faith for healing by someone laying hands on you. If that were the case, I would be the first in line! If you want faith, then hear the Word, read the Word, get the Word in you, and obey the Word.

On several occasions, during conferences or meetings, I've had the opportunity to meet authors of some of the books that have been given to me. Some ended up piled in a corner of my office, unread. At least I can tell these authors, "Oh, I have your book." But after spending a few days with them, listening to stories about their ministries, their families, and their lives in general, I feel like I want to actually read their books. What I might have considered subject matter of little interest to me now takes on new meaning, becomes relevant and noteworthy, because I have come to know the author.

The Holy Spirit is the Bible's Author, so if you're having trouble understanding it, ask the Author! When you read a book, you don't have the luxury of asking the writer to come and sit with you and explain or expound on what he has written. But with the Bible, you can! He will help you learn the deep truths of the Word, bring it alive, and give you a hunger to know even more.

What Did You Expect?

In Mark 2:3-12, we read the following story:

> *They came to Him [Jesus], bringing a paralytic who was carried by four men. And when they could not come near Him because of the crowd, they uncovered the roof where He was. So when they had broken through, they let down the bed on which the paralytic was lying. When Jesus saw their faith, He said to the paralytic, "Son, your sins are forgiven you...arise, take up your bed, and go to your house." Immediately he arose....*

I read this passage a while ago, and I heard the Holy Spirit ask me, "Can people *see* your faith?" Faith is intangible, but it can be seen in our actions and in our words. Jesus saw the faith of these four men, because they put their faith into action.

Jesus said to the paralytic, *"Son, your sins are forgiven you."* What did that have to do with anything? This man had come for physical healing, not forgiveness of sins. This really upset the religious people, because if Jesus claimed to have the power to forgive sins it meant that He claimed to be God.

They didn't have to say a thing. Jesus knew what they were thinking and asked them, *"Which is easier, to say to the paralytic 'Your sins are forgiven you,' or to say, 'Arise, take up your bed and walk?'"* (verse 9). Jesus wanted to show them that, because He is the Son of God, He could not only heal this man physically but spiritually as well. To Him, the greater miracle was spiritual.

Although the religious leaders of Jesus' day questioned His ability and authority to forgive sins, for many of us today, it's the other way around. Most of us have no trouble believing that Jesus saves. We don't seem to struggle with the "bigger" miracle. But what is much smaller in comparison—the physical—seems difficult for us to believe. We reason within ourselves, "Maybe God doesn't want to heal; maybe it's not God's will to heal."

As believers, we have full confidence in the miracle of salvation. When we offer the salvation message, we make bold statements such as, "No matter who you are, what you have done or where you have been, you can come to Jesus and He will receive you. You can pray and the blood of Jesus ***will*** wash you clean. Your name ***will*** be written in the Book of Life. You ***will*** be a brand new person."

But when it comes to physical healing, a lot of believers lose their certainty. If they don't say it, they at least think things like, "I know God heals some people, *but* maybe it's not His will to heal you," or, "Sure, God has healed others, *but* I've never really seen God heal someone with your condition." So their *"prayer of faith"* is more like, "Let's give it a try and see what happens!"

Can you imagine if I gave an altar call at the end of a service and said, "I know there are some of you who are not right with God. Now, He saves some people, but I'm not sure whether or not He wants to save you. You are really a hard case—a big sinner. You need to know that there are some in our midst that believe that God placed your sin, unbelief and disobedience there to teach you something. You also need to know that I've prayed for some people to be saved, and it didn't happen. But just come and pray; you never know..." I wouldn't see many people responding to such an uncertain invitation!

The reason altar calls for salvation are always positive and full of assurance is that preachers of the gospel believe God's Word. They believe that *"Whoever calls on the name of the LORD shall be saved."*[6] They believe that *"The blood of Jesus Christ His Son cleanses us from all sin."*[7]. They believe that *"If anyone hears My voice and opens the door* [of his or her heart], *I* [Jesus] *will come in."* [8] Why do they believe? Because the Bible tells them so!

Believers choose to accept what the Word of God says when it comes to salvation, yet some decide that the Word doesn't necessarily apply when it comes to sickness and disease, even though the Bible is filled with God's promises for healing. We, as God's people, must be as emphatic, as sure and as positive about physical healing as we are about spiritual healing.

Go Find Out!

In the early seventies, I was invited to be a guest on a secular phone-in radio program, hosted by a man by the name of Bill Roberts. He was an on-air personality who could really get people worked up by his outspoken and sometimes controversial opinions. Some people tried to deter me from appearing on this show because Bill had demonstrated a negative bias against guests or listener comments that were "religious." But I felt the Spirit of God telling me to go.

I would have liked to have spent some time visiting with Bill before the program, so that I could at least establish some rapport with him, but that wasn't possible because Bill was already on the air by the time I arrived at the station. I was escorted into the studio during a commercial break. It was a tiny room with only a little table, two chairs and a microphone in it. I shook his hand when I entered, and immediately we were on the air.

He introduced me to the listeners, set the tone of the program, making it clear he wasn't a believer, and took a few calls. Towards the end of another commercial break, he surprised me by saying, "I'm going to ask you to pray for people on the air." Before I could respond, he pressed the button and we were back on. He told the listeners to call in if they wanted me to pray for them. The lines instantly lit up. I felt I was really being put on the spot, but I prayed for each one who called with a request.

As I prayed, the callers began to report instantaneous healings. It was obvious Bill was getting increasingly agitated. Finally he admitted, "Okay, I'll admit it seems prayer works for some, but only for those who believe."

Since Bill had made it clear he didn't believe in God or the Bible, I said, "It also works for people who don't." It occurred to me that he was struggling to ask me something, so I said, "Do you need healing?"

He answered hesitantly, "I'm crippled with arthritis."

Because he'd been sitting the entire time we'd been together, I hadn't realized how severe his condition was. I also knew there were a lot of Christians listening and praying. I asked him, "How are you feeling right now?"

He told me he would have to walk up the steps outside the studio to find out how well he was doing. So I said, "Go find out." He put a caller on the line for me to chat with, and he left. When he came back, he grabbed the microphone and said, "It didn't work! It's still there!"

I heard myself saying, "Bill, I haven't prayed for you yet! Now that you've confirmed for everybody that the arthritis is still there, both you and the listeners will know when God indeed heals you!"

Right there, live on the radio, I prayed for him. He was uncomfortable with the whole thing. When I finished, I asked him to go try the stairs again. He was hesitant to do it, but since there were people listening, he reluctantly agreed. Again, he put a caller on the line for me and went out.

When he returned, his face was as white as a sheet. With his hands shaking, he took the microphone and said, "It's gone! All the pain is gone!"

I said to him, "You asked me to pray for you, and now you are healed. Now you need to praise God for healing you."

So, with hands still shaking, he said very timidly, "Praise God." A Christian listener called immediately and said, "Bill Roberts, it's so good to hear you praising the Lord!"

I had wonderful opportunities to not only pray for people for healing but to freely share the gospel message as well. After the program, I told him, "Bill, I don't want to push you, but if I were you, I would do some serious thinking about what we've been talking about today."

The following morning I turned on the radio to hear the morning announcers talking about Bill Roberts' healing. Shortly afterward, the station manager called me in and said, "This has really shaken things up here."

Bill Roberts and I became friends, and he'd often drop by my office for a visit. A while later, after making a decision to run for government office in an upcoming election, he came to see me. I began talking about his political campaign and other general things, but he interrupted me. "I don't want to discuss the campaign or work or the weather; I came here to tell you that I want to be a Christian, but I don't know how."

A miracle can change peoples' attitudes very quickly. I didn't have to push him—he came to me. That day, I had the privilege of praying with him and leading him to Christ. He asked Jesus to come into his life, to fill the void and make the necessary changes. When he finished praying, he gave me a big hug and said, "I love you!"

I said, "Since you've just started out in your Christian walk, I want to be there for you. I'm going to give you my home phone number. Any time you want to talk, just give me a call." When I made this offer, I didn't realize that his day usually started very early in the morning and that he would be calling me regularly at 5 a.m. just to let me know he was doing all right!

Bill's miraculous healing is a prime example of the impact it can make on unbelievers.

The Basics

To have an effective healing ministry, there are a few things you need to understand:

1) God hears prayers.

I've heard far too many mature Christians making statements such as "God doesn't speak to me any more. He doesn't hear me. It's as if my prayers are bouncing off the ceiling, so why should I pray?"

1 John 5:14 says, *"Now this is the confidence that we have in Him, that if we ask anything according to His will, He hears us."* Can a statement be any more certain or encouraging? You must understand that every time you pray for the sick, or anything else for that matter, God hears you. It's often when you're on the brink of breakthrough that the devil will try to discourage you and tell you that God isn't listening.

Persist in prayer, and refuse to give in to the enemy's lies telling you to stop. God is listening, and He hears you every time!

2) God promises to answer.

The answer may come instantly or gradually, but either way, God does answer the prayer of faith. John reminds us, *"If we know that He **hears** us, whatever we ask, we know that we **have** the petitions that we have asked of Him."*[9]

Our ministry has been based in Ottawa, Canada, for almost thirty years, and every once in a while a local newspaper or television station will do a report on us. One such time, a newspaper sent a young man to interview me.

From the beginning, this reporter's skepticism was very apparent, but since his superior had given him the assignment, he had no choice but to complete it. I told him, "I'll make you a deal. For every service you attend, I'll sit down with you and give you an interview." He reluctantly agreed but made it very clear that he didn't believe any of "this stuff" and that he had everything "figured out" already.

Three services and three interviews later, he admitted that he couldn't deny that people were actually being healed. I teased him and said, "But you told me prayer was nothing!"

He answered, "Yeah, well, forget about that. I might as well be honest. This experience has really messed me up!"

Here's why. Before each service, this young reporter would randomly select people who were coming in and ask them if they were going to be prayed for and what their physical need was. During the service, he would watch these specific people receive healing for the conditions they'd told him about. There were so many such incidents that he knew it could not be some kind of pre-arranged scheme or set-up. He became convinced that God really did answer prayer.

In Matthew 21:22 Jesus says, *"And whatever things you ask in prayer, believing, you will receive."* Sometimes, when praying for the sick, believers who aren't sure that God will answer pray long prayers. I think they're afraid to stop, because they dread the thought of looking at the sick person only to find they weren't healed. Or they finish the prayer by saying, "God, if it's Your will," because that seems like a good "out" if nothing happens.

God is looking for people who just believe that He not only hears prayer but answers them too!

When people come to you for prayer, you have the ability to either build up their faith or discourage them. If someone tells us, "I've just come from the doctor, and I've been diagnosed with such-and-such a disease," we can't reply by saying, "Oh dear, my uncle had that same disease and he died!" Although your uncle might have died from that same condition, speaking it to that person at that moment would obviously discourage their faith. The fact that your uncle died of the same disease isn't the criteria for praying the prayer of faith. It should make you even more determined, spurring you on to see this person totally healed. It's a kick in the devil's face!

I met a young man named Eric a few years ago He was a student at a ministry school where I was often asked to speak. The promise and anointing on his life were very evident. It was obvious to me and to many others that God had destined him for an amazing life of ministry.

He had a small lump on the back of his neck, and occasionally he'd ask me to pray for that lump to go away. I must confess, I prayed rather casually until a few months later, when I became aware of the seriousness of his situation. I was ministering at a healing conference that he attended with his parents. He looked deathly ill and explained to me that he had Hodgkin's disease. I took it to heart and prayed fervently for him then and faithfully each day in my prayer times.

After the conference, I kept in touch with him and his parents. I even travelled to Texas where he lived, just to serve Eric communion and pray with him. The healing didn't come. In early January, Eric's parents called to inform me that he had passed away.

I was completely devastated. I had been so sure that he would be healed.

That bitter experience started me on a journey. I began to devour the Word, searching every passage of Scripture dealing with healing and health, until I became convinced beyond a shadow of a doubt that it is always God's will to heal.

From then on, nothing would deter me. Satan had stolen Eric's life before he could fulfill his God-given destiny. I pasted a photograph of Eric on the flyleaf of my Bible and every time I look at his face, it shouts out to me, "Don't let any more lives be lost!"

Years later, at a healing service in England, a lady came forward and told me that she had Hodgkin's disease. She too had a large lump on her neck. I immediately thought of Eric and something rose up within me. A righteous anger consumed me as I heard the words, "Don't let any more lives be lost!" Without a moment's hesitation, I laid my hands on this woman's neck and prayed. This time, the enemy lost. She shouted, "The lump is gone! I'm healed!"

3) God can do anything.

The Bible says that the fruit of our lips should be the sacrifice of praise.[10] It does not just mean that we are to be people of praise, but that when we speak, our words must plant seeds of praise into people's hearts. When people are sick and weak, they often talk about their pain. We have the ability, the potential, to put something in their hearts that will produce praise.

Smith Wigglesworth[11] was a great man of faith who ministered in powerful healing ministry in the early 1900s. Part of his teaching included his belief that believers could never pray the prayer of faith if they were focused on the problem or the situation.

People sometimes feel they have to give me a complete medical history of their condition before I pray for them. But I find that the less I know, the easier it is to pray with expectation. My mind isn't distracted by the "impossibilities," and I can concentrate my heart on God's promises. And if the person has just rehearsed all the problems, their spirit will be filled with unbelief as well, instead of faith.

God has not called us to be medical experts! He has not called us to know everything! Like young David facing Goliath, He doesn't want us to be "giantologists"! God has called us to be experts in His power.

The apostle Paul set an example for us, saying, *"For I determined not to know anything among you except Jesus Christ and Him crucified"*[12] David also encouraged himself by declaring, *"My help comes from the LORD, Who made heaven and earth."*[13]

Doctors, counsellors and medicine have their limitations. Our real help comes from God—the God who created the universe. There is nothing that He cannot do. When take our eyes off the problem and fix them on Him, we know victory is sure!

I was scheduled to minister in India a few years ago, but before the departure date, a crisis developed in our ministry. I felt I needed to stay home and take care of the problem, but since I'd already made the commitment to the ministry in India, I had no choice but to go.

Throughout the entire plane trip I thought about the crisis. I was worrying. The more I focussed on the problem, the bigger it seemed to become. By the time I arrived at my destination, I was so discouraged that I had even begun thinking about quitting. I just wanted to get to my room and wallow in my sorrow.

But the leaders of the mission where I was staying told me, "The children have prepared some songs for you." I was not really in the mood for songs, but I felt I had to go because the children (two hundred of them) had made a big banner and were all excited a about the special welcome they had planned for me.

None of the children spoke English, but they had worked

very hard learning to sing two songs phonetically in my language, just for me. They lined up in two rows outside the mission house, boys on one side, girls on the other, all with big smiles on their faces. With their cute little accents they sang a children's song containing these words: "My God is so big, so strong and so mighty; there's nothing my God cannot do..." Then, as they came to the close of the song, they sang, "There's nothing that He cannot do—for you!" and two hundred kids pointed their fingers at me! Suddenly, I realized I had been looking at the situation from the wrong perspective. I had been thinking about what the enemy had done. But at that moment, I realized, "My God is so big!" It took two hundred Indian kids to help me see that, from God's point of view, this mountain was nothing more than a molehill!

We will never pray the prayer of faith unless this truth sinks in: "*Whatever things you ask when you pray, believe that you receive them, and you will have them.*"[14] The only way to believe is to put things in the right perspective and to focus on how big God is. God is bigger than any disease. God is bigger than any pain.

4) He paid the price.

The price for healing has been paid—totally and absolutely. Isaiah 53:5 says, "*by His stripes we are healed.*" That was before Jesus' death on the cross, looking forward to the day the price would be paid. Peter referred to the finished work of Christ when he said, "*By* [His] *stripes you were healed.*"[15]

Some people may argue that Peter was talking about spiritual healing. If that were the case, what then do you do with 1 Corinthians 6:20, "*You were bought at a price; therefore glorify God* ***in your body*** *and in your spirit,* *which are God's"* (emphasis added)? Jesus paid the price for the healing of our bodies *and* our spirits.

When you pray for someone to be healed, you have to understand that you are praying for something that is paid for already. You don't need to beg; it is yours—you just have to take it. You have to lay claim to your rightful inheritance.

When you buy something in a store, you're given a receipt. The receipt is the proof (the evidence) that you, in fact, have paid. Likewise, healing has been paid for, and the Bible is your receipt.

You need to get this in your spirit. Knowing that Jesus paid the price for your absolute healing is necessary if you are going to pray with any kind of assurance at all. Otherwise, your prayer won't be a prayer of faith; it will be more like "hoping for the best" or "keeping your fingers crossed."

When you know that God is listening, you will pray with authority—authority that has nothing to do with your personality, background or education. It has been paid for, so you are free to take it.

When Moses sent spies to Canaan, they came back with conflicting reports. The people began to fear what would happen if they tried to enter the land. Caleb stood before them and challenged them. In essence, he asked, "Whose report are you going to believe? Yes, there are challenges, but God is on our side!"[16] When circumstances and symptoms seem to be in contradiction with the Word of God, choose to believe the Word, *not* the symptoms.

Jesus said in Matthew 17:20, *"If you have faith...nothing will be impossible for you."* And in John 15:7, He declared, *"If you abide in Me, and My words abide in you, you will ask what you desire, and it shall be done for you."* I choose to believe Jesus!

Doubt Your Doubts!

If you have questions, something you don't understand, ask God. He knows your thoughts anyway, so you might as well be honest with Him. The great men and women of God in the Bible were absolutely honest with God. Why should you pretend that everything is fine and dandy when you can openly and honestly ask God to help?

There are many people who receive a miraculous touch from the Lord, but later, sometimes months or years later, the symptoms turn up once again. That can be very confusing. It seems out of character for God to heal and then take it back, because when God does something, He does it perfectly. When He heals someone, it is for good, not just temporary. So why does His Word and their experience seem to be in conflict?

The answer lies in the fact that the enemy is a deceiver, the father of all lies. I don't believe that once God delivers you, the enemy can bring back the disease or the problem—unless you give him permission to do so.

How do you give him permission? I believe one way is by deliberately violating the proper care of your body. For instance, if you've been healed of a breathing condition caused by smoking, then you return to smoking, you give the enemy permission to attack your lungs again. Or if you were healed of problems related to poor eating habits, and you continue filling your body with junk, you're inviting him to attack you again.

Or he may create the symptoms similar to your previous condition, to make you doubt that the healing you experienced was real. In doubting, you open the door for the condition to return. You should treat these "phantom symptoms" the same way you'd deal with unwanted mail. Just as you'd write across the envelope "Return to Sender," you can do the same with symptoms. Refuse to accept them; mark on them "Return to Sender," and send them back to hell where they came from!

Not long ago, we had a wonderful healing service, and a lot of people received outstanding miracles. Many of them returned to their doctors and had their healings confirmed. There was, however, one lady with a lung disease who received a healing, but soon after, she began having symptoms again.

When I heard about her, I thought to myself, "If that lady had been surrounded by people of faith, they could have helped her stand and refuse the enemy's phantom symptoms." When ministering to people, you must make certain they know that the healing they receive is sure, that it's unconditional, that it's a free gift of God, and that they don't need to live in fear of the disease returning.

Unfortunately, many preachers put all of the onus on the recipient—"If you have enough faith, you will be healed. If you don't get healed, it's because you don't have enough faith." Although faith is a key component, it must be heartbreaking to God when believers place condemnation on others. They simply need encouragement to relax and enjoy His gifts, not fret and worry all the time that the symptoms might come back or that they don't have enough faith to keep the healing.

When I first came to Jesus, I thought I had to hang on to Him for dear life; otherwise, He would let go of me. But the Scriptures tell us that God keeps us securely in the palm of His hand.[17] Healing is just as sure.

I remember hearing Kathryn Kuhlman say that it broke her heart to see how people thought they could lose God's grace, that they had to do something to earn His love and healing touch. The Father's heart is such that He will never give and then take away.

James 1:6,7 says,

> *"Let him ask in faith, with no doubting, for he who doubts is like a wave of the sea driven and tossed by the wind. For let not that man suppose that he will receive anything from the Lord."*

That is exactly what many of us believers do. We waver, unsure whether or not God really wants to heal us. But the Church must rise up and take authority. When the devil tries to discourage you by asking, "Who do you think you are?" answer with assurance, "I know who I am. I am a member of *the 'chosen generation, a royal priesthood.'*[18] God has given me the keys: whatever I bind is bound. Whatever I loose is loosed!"[19] Dare to believe God's Word!

Broadcast It!

When God heals you, it is very important to give Him glory. God lives in people's praises. We are often quick to talk about our problems to others, but it is far more important, and much more edifying, for us to give the Lord credit when a miracle happens.

Have you noticed that the enemy always wants us to focus on what has *not* happened? Why not focus on what *has* happened, and give God glory for what He's done—even the smallest improvement in your health—and for what He is going to do!

Recently, I taught about healing in a large Spirit-filled church. Afterwards the pastor told me, "That was the best teaching I've ever heard about healing!" I was feeling just a little pleased with myself, until he added, "Come to think of it, I don't remember *ever* having heard a teaching about healing before!" That brought me back down to size!

But it also pointed out one of the reasons more people don't receive healing.

Faith comes by hearing, and hearing by the Word of God.[20] The Word of God regarding healing must become an important element of what is preached from the pulpits of our nation! It is time to become obsessed with faith in His Word and to cause extreme damage to the kingdom of darkness!

---

1 Romans 4:18.

2 Ephesians 3:20, emphasis added.

3 Matthew 7:7.

4 Genesis 18:14.

5 Romans 10:17.

6 Acts 2:21.

7 1 John 1:7.

8 Revelation 3:20.

9 1 John 5:15, emphasis added.

10 Hebrews 13:15.

11 Smith Wigglesworth, *The Complete Collection of His Life Teachings*, compiled by Roberts Liardon, (Tulsa: Albury Publishing, 1997).

12 1 Corinthians 2:2.

13 Psalms 121:2.

14 Mark 11:24.

15 1 Peter 2:24, emphasis added.

16 Numbers 13:30.

[17] Psalm 139:10.
[18] 1 Peter 2:9.
[19] Matthew 16:19.
[20] Romans 10:17.

Chapter Six

Six Keys to Breakthrough

No one has it all figured out when it comes to healing. I'm always a little nervous around someone who thinks he has all the answers. However, over the course of more than thirty years of healing ministry, I've learned many valuable lessons as I've dug into the Word and its truths concerning healing.

That's why I recently wrote a book entitled *Six Keys to Breakthrough in Healing*. It isn't by any means an exhaustive list, but I believe it contains several important insights into why some people don't seem to see the results they are praying for. In the following pages, I will provide just a quick overview of these six keys. The complete teaching is in *Six Keys to Breakthrough In Healing*, but I thought it important to touch on them here.

1. Confess your trespasses...that you may be healed" (James 5:16, emphasis added).

Job's friends, who were supposedly trying to comfort him, told him that all his troubles were because he had sin in his life. Although Job continued to search his heart, the fact of the matter was, the devastating events that transpired were not as a result of sin at all.[1]

Your friends might be the same as Job's. The moment they see that you're not getting any better, they assume that there must be sin in your life. Job's friends were way off base, and your friends could very well be too. If you know your heart is right with God and nothing is separating you from Him, you can rest assured.

But you do have to understand that, according to James, healing is hindered by unconfessed sin. Oftentimes believers expect to receive healing but refuse to deal with the sin in their lives. God's promise of healing is for believers who live according to His ways.

I urge you to use as much tact as you can in approaching someone with this. The only ones who truly knows if there is unconfessed sin is the person and God Himself. You can't point your finger and accuse them of such things. Instead of condemning them, however, gently suggest that they ask the Holy Spirit to search their hearts for any sin that might be hindering. There might even be something there that they are totally unaware of. Assure them, however, that if they have already confessed it, they are forgiven, and God will not ever remember it against them again!

Isaiah 59:1, 2 tells us,

"Behold the Lord's hand is not shortened, That it cannot save; Nor His ear heavy, That it cannot hear.

But your iniquities have separated you from your God; And your sins have hidden His face from you, So that He will not hear."

James 5:16 tells us the same thing, but with a positive approach, *"The effective, fervent prayer of a righteous man avails much."*

Once sin is confessed, the hindrance is gone. The blockage has been removed. This is an important point to remember, because many times when you lay hands on people, the devil reminds them of their sins, discouraging them and making them feel "unworthy." We need to be constantly on guard, deflecting his lies. The Bible tells us that once sin is confessed, the blockage is gone!

2. *"**Honor your father and your mother,** that your days may be long upon the land"* (Exodus 20:12, emphasis added).

According to this verse, refusing to honour your parents means a short, unfulfilled life. Please note here that God doesn't allow any qualifications to honouring your parents. He doesn't say, "If your parents loved you and never did anything to hurt you, then honour them." It has nothing to do with us, or with them. Rather, it has everything to do with God. He has given us a conditional promise of a long, full life. Our part is to simply give honour to our parents.

Now, I know that it's easy for me to say that because I had wonderful parents who loved me as a child. I never lacked for anything emotionally. I also know, however, that there are many people who have suffered terrible abuse and hurt from their parents. How could they possibly honour their fathers and mothers?

A few years ago, after speaking in a service about the Father's heart, I had the congregation sing the children's song, "Jesus loves me; this I know." Many of the people there were genuinely moved by the simple message. One lady in particular approached me and told me that she had been sexually abused by her father.

She continued, with tears welling up in her eyes, telling how, after he would leave her bedroom, she would go to her closet, feeling so dirty and worthless, cover herself with a blanket and whisper the words, "Jesus loves me; this I know, for the Bible tells me so. Little ones to Him belong; they are weak, but He is strong." Over and over she would sing this whispered song until she finally fell asleep.

This horrendous abuse began when she was only six years old and continued every night for years. I couldn't even imagine the hurt she must have felt, the pain and heartache. The very man who was should have protected her violated her instead. I just stood there, feeling so broken by her story as she continued and asked, "Based on your sermon today, you're telling me that God loves my father?"

I answered as gently and with as much care as I could, "God can't stop loving anybody. God *is* love. His love doesn't depend on whether we are good or bad. He just loves."

"Are you telling me, then, that I have to love my father too?" she asked.

I looked at her kindly and said, "I can't imagine how badly you hurt. But at some point, for your sake, you have to come to the point where you forgive and honour your father. To do otherwise, continuing to hold resentment and anger towards him, will only hurt you."

That young lady had a real breakthrough with Father God that morning and took a giant step towards living a long, full life. Although we don't often associate the two,

God's Word tells us that in order to live a long healthy life, we must honour our father and mother.

*"**Husbands...**[give] **honor to the wife...**that your prayers may not be hindered"*(1 Peter 3:7, emphasis added).

Continuing on with the subject of honour, we see that Peter in this passage gives us another key to healing. If you want to have an effective prayer life—receiving healing, plus praying for the sick and seeing miracles—you can't be one person at home and another outside. Our prayers will not be effective if we don't honour our spouse.

The way some men treat their wives in public is disgraceful—one can only imagine what goes on behind closed doors. As the saying goes, "Actions speak louder than words." If you truly respect your spouse, your actions will reflect it.

My father treated my mother very well, like a queen. I resolved in my heart, from a young age, that if God entrusted me with the wonderful gift of a wife, I would bless her and treat her like royalty, just like my dad had done. As it turns out, God did give me the best, and in keeping my word, I will always honour her.

David prayed, *"That I may daily perform my vows."*[2] In other words, David knew that there was a time he made a vow and gave his life to God. He didn't want to leave that promise in the past but committed to renew it every day, showing his devotion to God on a daily basis.

Gwen and I exchanged vows at the altar about forty years ago, but I try, in some way, to renew my vow to her every day, showing her that I love and honour her. There are many ways we can honour our spouse. It can be as simple as a kind word or gesture. You may be surprised by what an "I love you" or even a simple "thank you" means to your partner.

If you want to be a man or a woman of God, seeing miracles in your ministry and having your prayers go unhindered, you must commit to honouring your spouse.

3. *"Who is the man who desires life, And loves many days, that he may see good?* ***Keep your tongue from evil, And your lips from speaking deceit.*** *Depart from evil and do good; Seek peace and pursue it. The eyes of the LORD are on the righteous, And His ears are open to their cry. The face of the LORD is against those who do evil, To cut off the remembrance of them from the earth"* (Psalm 34:12-16, emphasis added).

Gossip and negative chit-chat about others in the body of Christ is an absolute no-no. Under no circumstances should you ever spread untruths or rumours about your brothers and sisters—at least not if you desire a long, healthy, prosperous life.

Let's say, for example, you catch your thumb in the car door. Do you yell at your thumb, "Stupid thumb! How could you be so ignorant and do such a thing?" Or do you say to your knee, "Hey, knee, I know that you care deeply about thumb and want to see the best for him, that's why you should know that, earlier today, I saw thumb get caught in the car door—again!"

No, your body wouldn't react like that at all! Instead, you would immediately react, pull the thumb out of harm's way, hold it close and shield it from further injury. That is how the body is designed to work—every part working together for the good of the whole. Think about it. We are the Body of Christ. How should we react when one of our members stumbles in their walk? Psalm 34:13 lays it out very clearly. *"Keep your tongue from evil, And your lips from speaking deceit."*

There isn't one person, preacher or minister who could ever be considered perfect, but to criticize and tear down people with our words will only hurt ourselves.

Do you want to see health and healing be a distinguishing characteristic of your life? When people introduce you, wouldn't it be nice to hear "This is the healthiest person I know"? Then you cannot, according to Scripture, 'bad-mouth' others in the Body.

If you discover a serious fault or failure in someone, there are steps you can take to address it, but I can assure you, gossip isn't among them.

I was told that years ago when a young Billy Graham was first starting out, he made a covenant with Cliff Barrows and George Beverly Shea. They agreed together that none of the three would ever speak negatively about another ministry, and if one of them did, the others could hold him accountable. I don't think it's a coincidence that the Billy Graham Evangelistic Association has since been one of the most steady, solid and consistent ministries in the world. Of course, there are many factors involved in this success, but I believe that this covenant agreement, made in the very early years, is one of the greatest.

Just as Israel was made up of many tribes, the body of Christ is made up of different types of people. When Joshua was leading the people into the Promised Land, he asked one man from each of the tribes of Israel to step into the Jordan River and pick a stone. They put these stones together in one place as a reminder for future generations of what God had done.[3] Some of the tribes didn't really get along, but by instructing these representative men to advance together, God was telling them that, in order to enter the Promised Land, they had to join hands and cross tribal lines.

We can accomplish a lot more together than we can separately. Many people were surprised when I partnered together with John Arnott, of the Toronto Airport Christian Fellowship, because he is from a different "tribe." The way I look at it, however, is that we both want to see people healed and saved, so why shouldn't I?

Not long ago, Gwen and I decided to travel to Vancouver to attend a conference conducted by Kenneth and Gloria Copeland. Some of our friends were shocked. They asked us, "You're not into that *Word Faith* thing, are you?" My answer to them was, "We are into faith and we are into the Word, so what is the alternative?" We came away from the conference feeling injected with wonderful, positive truth. Kenneth Copeland may very well be from a "different tribe," but I refuse to speak poorly of him or his ministry; on the contrary, I will bless and uplift them every chance I get.

There are many diverse ministries, but I urge you, even if you dislike the personality or the ministry, look for the positive. I am constantly being told, "But Benny Hinn sensationalizes healing!" or "David Wilkerson is too strong—why can't he just relax?" or "Robert Schuller is way too into positive thinking!" My answer is always the same, "When you're reaching as many people as these men are, then come talk to me. Until then, if you can't say something nice, don't say anything at all!"

You will find good and bad in every ministry, but I urge you, look for the good. And when you find it, it will bless you and your life!

Never speak words that tear down. Instead, speak life. Build up your brother or sister with kind, God-filled words. That way, God, who is faithful to His Word, will open His ears to your cries. It's another key to your healing and health!

4. *"Forgive us our debts, as we **forgive** our **debtors**"* (Matthew 6:12, emphasis added).

In numerous instances throughout the Scriptures, we observe that answer to prayer hinges on atonement, making wrongs right, and having an attitude of forgiveness. Jesus Himself told us,

> *"If you bring your gift to the altar, and there remember that your brother has something against you, leave your gift there before the altar, and go your way. First be reconciled to your brother, and then come and offer your gift"* (Matthew 5:23,24).

In other words, if you are harbouring resentment and unforgiveness towards someone, don't even bother asking God for anything until you make things right.

Following the American Civil War, General Robert E. Lee visited a Kentucky woman who took him to the remains of what was once a grand old tree in front of her house. She cried as she told the general that the trunk and limbs of the tree had been destroyed by Federal artillery fire. She waited for Lee to respond with harsh words, condemning the Northern army; instead, he said, "Cut it down, my dear madam, and forget it. It is better to forgive the injustices of the past than to allow them to remain, let bitterness take root and poison the rest of our life..."[4]

Unforgiveness is a poison. It will do you no good to hold on to your anger. In fact, allowing your unforgiving spirit to control you will destroy what God intends to be a healthy life. In all honesty, the *only* person you will hurt is yourself. That is not a cliché; it's the truth.

Karl Menninger, the famed psychiatrist, once said that if he could convince the patients in psychiatric hospitals that their sins were forgiven, 75 percent of them could walk out the next day![5] Unforgiveness will destroy you. Forgive, forget, and walk the rest of your days in healing!

5. ***Don't accept the illness!***

A woman came to me, asking me to pray for her. "What are you praying for?" I said.

"My arthritis," she replied.

"It's not your arthritis," I told her.

She looked at me as if I had accused her of stealing! She said, "I've had it for over twenty years. It it's not mine, then whose is it?"

I answered, "It's the devil's!"

She reacted by saying, "I didn't know the devil had arthritis!"

For years, she had been told that she had to live with this disease because there is no cure for arthritis. But when she grasped the truth I was giving her, she got upset with herself for having accepted this sickness from the enemy for so many years. I prayed for her, and she was completely healed.

Another woman, a believer, asked me to pray for her. She said, "I'm going to have a nervous breakdown." When I asked her what made her think that, she told me that her mother had one and her grandmother had one, so she was going to have one, too!

Doctors, friends, and even believers encourage us to accept things as they are. They tell us not to get our hopes up and to simply face facts. Jesus, however, is the greatest hope-builder I've ever met! All He had to feed a crowd of thousands were five loaves and two fish. He didn't tell them that it wasn't enough; He instructed his disciples to organize the people into groups of fifty and prepare to feed them. He was building their hopes up! And He delivered! We need to have a hope-building ministry, just like Jesus.

Be prepared, though. If you step out, refuse your sickness, and claim God's promises for your life, people are going to tell you to be "reasonable," face reality and accept your lot in life. Answer them by saying that the reality is that Jesus paid the price on the cross. *"By His stripes we are healed"* (Isaiah 53:5).

If you are battling sickness, recognize that it is not yours—it doesn't belong to you, so stop claiming ownership! Remember, mark it "Return to Sender." To hell with sickness!

7. *"**Bring all the tithes** into the storehouse, That there may be food in My house, And try Me now in this...If I will not open for you the windows of heaven And pour out for you such blessing That there will not be room enough to receive it"*(Malachi 3:10, emphasis added).

Rodney Howard Browne made this comment to me a few years ago: "I have never met anybody who flows consistently in anointing who is not a consistent giver."

I agree! All the people I know who are in miracle ministries are givers—always looking for ways to give.

Tithes and offerings are two separate things. A tithe is 10 percent of our earnings, given to the local church—the storehouse. Tithing is a very basic principle, as relevant to New Testament believers as it was to the Old Testament people. Jesus Himself encouraged people to tithe. If you don't think it is a New Testament practice, you could follow what the early Christians did, as recorded in the Book of Acts. They sold everything they had, and gave it!

If we don't pay our tithes, we are robbing God. That's

exactly what Malachi said in chapter 3, verse 8. "*Will a man rob God? Yet you have robbed Me! But you say, 'In what way have we robbed You?' In tithes and offerings.*"

We cannot expect God to bless us in any way (including healing) if we are consistently stealing from Him. It would be as if I went to the corner store several times a week and took anything I chose—as the owner watched—and never paid. Then, suppose several weeks later I ran into financial trouble and went to the storeowner, asking him for help. He'd say, "How dare you! I've watched you for weeks, stealing from me!" That's what we're doing to God when we use the tithe that belongs to him. Malachi 3:9 goes on to say "*You are cursed with a curse, For you have robbed Me, Even this whole nation.*"

Now, the flip side of it is that God blesses people who tithe, allowing them to live and flow in anointing so that they can minister and be strong. According to Malachi 3, we Christians have the ability, the authority, to open the windows of heaven. And God will pour out such blessing that we will not be able to contain it! This "overwhelming" blessing comes only when we start giving.

I don't know about you, but I want the windows of heaven to open over my life and ministry! When the windows are open—get ready for a miracle!

When we pray for someone and don't see breakthrough, it may be because they are not tithing. If they don't, they need to understand that their refusal will shut the windows of heaven.

If, having gone through the six keys to breakthrough in healing, you still haven't seen the results, do what Ephesians 6:13 says, "*Having done all...stand.*" Just stand. You do your part, and you can expect God to do His part. Stand.

---

[1] Job 4-6.

[2] Psalm 61:8.

[3] Joshua 4:1-9.

[4] Charles Bracelen Flood, Lee: *The Last Years* (Mariner Books, 1998).

[5] *Today in the Word*, March 1989, p.8.

Chapter Seven

Do You Want It?

Lately, I've been asking people, "Do you believe God is going to do something great in our nation?" Most of them respond with an emphatic "Yes!" So, then I ask, "Do you believe God is going to use *you*?" Most people are more than a little taken aback. It's one thing to believe God's going to do something. It's a whole different thing to realize He wants to use them.

Recently, Gwen and I where ministering in Wales and really got the impression that the church there was earnestly expecting the same type of nation-wide revival that swept across their land in 1904.

I made an announcement that momentarily stunned the group that had gathered for the meeting. "Evan Roberts is dead, and he's not coming back!" I said. "Smith

Wigglesworth and Kathryn Kuhlman are dead too! If Wales is going to see revival again, it will be through you. God wants to use *you*!"

Some of them looked absolutely devastated. But it's true! Each one of us can be used by God. He doesn't expect extraordinary faith or talent. He is simply looking for someone to say "Here I am—use me!" He is looking for "willing" people.

I've met people who feel unworthy to be used of God. They say they aren't Bible-college trained, or they aren't smart enough, or their past was too horrendous. Maybe you've got some of the same concerns.

But God's not concerned about your worthiness. He made you worthy and gave you His authority! You are His child, and if you simply decide to walk in faith and obedience, you are a candidate for carrying out His healing ministry.

I'm Humble—and Proud of It!

I'm urging you be careful, because the same devil that told you that you're not worthy will turn around and whisper, "Wow, did you see what God just did through you? You must be really something for God to use you like that! You're probably more anointed than your pastor. He certainly didn't see the results you did—and you're so humble about it!"

If you believe the enemy's lies, you'll begin operating in your own strength, or, instead of giving God glory, you'll begin taking it for yourself. That will thwart your effectiveness and cause your anointing to vanish.

Early in my ministry, people kept telling me how humble they thought I was. After hearing it over and over, I became proud of my humility! The Lord had to bring me down a peg or two, until I learned to trust Him and rely totally on His anointing if I was going to remain effective.

Please don't pay attention to the people who'll tell you that they think you have more anointing than the pastor and the evangelist. Listening to "compliments" like that will lead you into very dangerous territory. Once that seed is planted, coming under any kind of godly authority will be a very difficult thing for you.

The enemy of your soul would love for you to "do your own thing." But the end result will be spiritual shipwreck. The anointing and gifts He entrusted to you, the touch of His glory on your life, will be lost if you allow pride to grow in your life. You must be part of the Body of Christ. You can't function *in* Him if you're not connected *to* Him!

Even though I'm an evangelist, I too have to be part of the Body of Christ. I'm part of a local church in Ottawa, with a leadership team and governing board that submits to our denominational overseers. I subject myself to several levels of accountability—men and women of God who have the right to correct, exhort and challenge me. I need that.

Our evangelistic association also has a board of directors, which makes the major decisions. At first, I thought a board was restrictive, but I soon came to realize that it is necessary. They are there to help me reach my destination, to fulfill our God-given purpose and vision. They are like train tracks that keep me headed in the right direction. Since the board is made up of people who have one vision—to see this nation shaken for God—I submit to them.

As believers we are all part of one Body. If we try to force things, make things happen outside the parameters of the Body of Christ, we thwart what God has for us. The devil will do everything he can to sever ministries from the

Body. At first, he'll tell you that you're not worthy to be used for ministry; then, if you ignore him and let God use you, he'll try to separate you from the Body, to make you think that you are better than others.

Either of these attitudes can and will destroy what God wants to do through you. Remember who you are and where you've come from; remember that you are totally reliant on the grace of God and the redemptive work of Christ.

I am convinced that you can never have authority if you never learn to submit to authority. Just imagine what it must have been like for young David. After he was anointed to be king,[1] he went back home to look after his father's sheep![2]

Many believers find submission a very difficult thing. They don't want to be restricted by rules or under someone else's authority. But I ask you, can a train go anywhere without being on its tracks?

From Cleaning to Healing!

My first mentor in ministry followed this philosophy: If you are not prepared to clean the toilets, then you're not prepared to stand behind the pulpit. It is true! You cannot have any kind of ministry if you're not willing to serve people.

The early believers in the book of Acts could have refused to serve tables, to care for hungry widows, claiming they had been anointed for "ministry" and not such menial tasks. They were willing to serve in the "unglamorous" positions, however, and as a result, people were healed.

If I took along all the people who have ever told me they are called to be evangelists and asked to travel with me, I'd have to charter a fleet of jumbo jets! Once, for instance, when I was in the Arctic, a young man approached me and said, "I believe God has called me to be an evangelist. I want to go with you, travel with you and learn from you." I answered, "I believe you, but you need to stay here and do whatever your pastor needs you to do—and do it with all your might! Ask him to let you do what no one else wants to do."

This poor young man couldn't understand how all this could help him be an evangelist and heal the sick! He was devastated. He had never learned to serve at home, so he was not ready to minister elsewhere.

I explained to him that when David was summoned to the palace, all he was asked to do was to play music and soothe Saul's spirit. The Scripture says, "*David came to Saul and entered his service.*"[3] Even though he knew he was the true anointed king, he served Saul.

In the book of Acts, all the believers had a miracle ministry. People who served tables had a miracle ministry. Deacons had miracle ministries. God wants the book of Acts to happen once again, and I believe the latter is going to be far greater than the former!

There are three things we can learn from people in the Bible who did great things for God.

1. Know Who God Is

The Body of Christ is filled with people who don't really know the character of God. If we say "God has brought this sickness on me," we don't know God. If we say "God has sent this illness to teach me something," then we don't know God at all! He can turn cursing into blessing. He is good. It is as simple as that.

If you'd asked Moses what God is like, he'd have said, "Sit down, it's going to take a while, because I'm going to tell you about my best friend."

If you'd asked Enoch what God is like, he would have said, "I can tell you, because I was just walking with him."

The Bible says, *"The people who know their God shall be strong, and carry out great exploits."*[4] The Holy Spirit has come to help us know our God—that's why He's here. All you have to do is ask Him to help you know God more, and He will. The world may not recognize Him, but we'll know Him, because He lives in us. God Almighty has taken up residence within us. How amazing!

The enemy will do whatever he can to discourage and distract you—to try to get you off course—but hang in there! If the attacks seem to be relentless, get excited. Take it as a personal compliment! What that says is the enemy has more confidence in you than you have in yourself.

The enemy considers you a threat. He doesn't waste his time attacking people who are not going to do anything for God. So, be encouraged. The Bible tells us that *"David encouraged himself in the LORD, his God."*[5]

In I Samuel 30, we see David, a great man of God, doing God's work. He and his mighty men were fighting the enemy on behalf of God's people. After a hard-fought battle, they returned home one day, only to discover that during their absence, the enemy had come and laid waste to their hometown, Ziklag. Their houses were destroyed, their families taken hostage, and all of their possessions stolen.

Isn't that amazing? There are a lot of preachers who will tell you that if you serve God faithfully, He'll bless you, and your life will be "smooth sailing." David had served God, obeyed Him and gave all he had to Him. That day, however, he found out that, in spite of all he'd done and given, he had lost everything.

What would you do if your whole world fell apart while you were obeying God and working for Him? The Scripture says, *"David encouraged himself in the* LORD." He didn't encourage himself by looking at the ruins of his house—that would have been discouraging! He didn't encourage himself by reminding himself continually what the enemy had done to his family—that would have been discouraging. Instead, he let God's presence comfort him.

If you constantly focus on what the enemy has done—talk and think about it all the time—you are magnifying the works of the enemy.

Imagine this scenario. A successful, active couple are in their prime. Suddenly the young husband begins to experience severe pain and other troublesome symptoms. He goes to the doctor and receives the devastating news that he has a rare disease.

Since they know nothing about this disease, they go to every Web site available to research the subject. They purchase books describing the condition and consult as many experts as possible, in an effort to learn everything they can about the disease. All the information tells them the condition is hopeless.

The couple is overwhelmed and discouraged. Every shred of hope for the future is shattered. They find it nearly impossible to believe God for healing. As they fret and worry, his condition quickly deteriorates.

Suddenly it occurs to them that they are going about their research all wrong. They decide to turn off the computer and open the Bible. They look in the concordance to see if the disease is listed and find no reference to it at all. So they look up *diseases* and find a verse that reads, "[He] *heals all your diseases.*"[6] *All* includes his condition! Their despair turns to hope, and they believe God for his total healing!

All includes any disease you may be concerned about! No sickness, diagnosis, symptom or physical attack should cause you to lose a moment's sleep. Be encouraged! The battle is the Lord's.

We live in an amazing day when knowledge on any subject under the sun is at our fingertips. There's even been a phrase added to our vocabulary as a result—"information overload." It has become so easy to research symptoms and diagnose ourselves that many Christians jump on-line before even consulting what the Bible might have to say about the condition.

Instead of studying up on an illness or disease, why don't you study what the Word says? Turn to Isaiah 53:4,5:

> *"Surely He has borne our griefs And carried our sorrows; Yet we esteemed Him stricken, Smitten by God, and afflicted. But He was wounded for our transgressions, He was bruised for our iniquities; The chastisement for our peace was upon Him, And by His stripes we are healed."*

That would be an excellent place to start. Instead of learning about the disease, learn about God's promises concerning your healing. Become an expert on how great God is!

Let's go back to David. While he was looking at the ruins of his house, his "loyal" men began to discuss how to kill him, blaming him for their loss. That would have been quite discouraging! But he kept his focus right. He kept encouraging himself in the Lord.

Perhaps there was a time you reached out to someone to bless and minister to. Then the time came when you had a need, only to have them turn their back on you. Just when you needed them, they abandoned you. The Bible says, "*David encouraged himself in the LORD.*"

Like David, we must find our joy, our strength and our encouragement in the Lord. If we come to know our God, we will also come know that He is great and awesome; nothing else matters; we can't give up.

When everyone else was ready to give up, David couldn't, because he knew His God. When you know God, you can't quit. When you know God, you can't get discouraged. You make the decision to look toward Him, not the circumstances. It is an act of your will: "*I will lift up mine eyes unto the hills, from whence cometh my help.*"[7]

It never ceases to amaze me. When we are in an airplane, no matter how bad the weather may be, no matter how foggy, how cloudy, how rainy, as soon as we break through the clouds, the sun is always shining! In the same way, no matter how bleak your situation is, know that God is there, ready and willing to heal.

David said to himself, "I'm going a little higher! I choose to take my eyes off my surroundings, and I **will** lift up my eyes unto the hills. That is where my help comes from. It doesn't come from organizations. It doesn't come from people around me. It doesn't come from the lending institution or the counsellor. "*My help comes from the LORD, Who made heaven and earth.*"[8] In other words, David was saying, "If my God is big enough to make heaven and earth, then my problem, in comparison, is small. If my God is big enough to speak a word and create a universe, if my God is big enough to make the mountains, then the miracle I need is small." Thinking of God's greatness, instead of the problem, will always encourage and strengthen you.

2. Know Who You Are

Some time ago, a young man made an appointment to come and see me in my office. I was quite pleased, thinking that I could encourage him by telling him some of the things the Lord had done for me and somehow touch his life. Little did I know that this man intended to "straighten me out"!

He had recently attended one of our healing meetings and was disturbed by a statement I had made. He challenged me by asking, "In the meeting the other night, I think I heard you say you were binding the power of the devil. Did you really say that?"

I answered, "Yes, I did."

He continued, "I think I also heard you say you were loosing the power of the Holy Spirit. Did I hear you correctly?"

"Yes," I answered once again.

He glared at me, disgusted, and asked, "Who do you think you are?"

I was so glad he asked! I answered, "The Bible says that in times past I was a sinner; I didn't count.[9] But no more! I am redeemed. I am a royal priesthood, a chosen generation.[10] I am the head and not the tail.[11] I am no longer a slave but a son.[12] When I am weak, I am made strong.[13] I have been given His authority, the keys of the kingdom, and whatever I bind on earth will be bound in heaven, and whatever I loose on earth will be loosed!"[14]

Trust me, I am fully aware of my inadequacies and limitations, but they're irrelevant! It's not my power or my authority that chases the demonic forces of sickness and disease. I simply know that He allows me to use His name, His power and His authority to destroy strongholds and see the miraculous! *"He who is in you is greater than he who is in the world."*[15]

3. Pursue, Hunger, Take

If you desire anointing to minister in healing power, don't allow yourself to be distracted. Friends might criticize you, your family may misunderstand you, but if your motives are pure and your heart yearns for His presence, you will receive what you desire.

Elisha received a double portion anointing because he *pursued* it tirelessly. He pressed on through Gilgal, pressed on through Bethel, pressed on through Jericho. He pressed on through the sons of the prophets' skepticism and saw Elijah taken to heaven.[16] He didn't want to miss the opportunity to receive everything God had for him.

That is the kind of persistence that can frustrate people around us. "Why can't you be satisfied with what you have?" they may say. But the more you get, the more you'll want. Don't be satisfied with where you are! Keep pressing! It's people who aren't satisfied with their present spiritual state that change the course of history.

On a recent trip to the UK, a young man approached me and said, "The last time you were here, you preached about the Holy Spirit, so I made a decision that day to actively pursue Him." He continued, "It hasn't worked. I haven't broken through, I haven't got it—I'm frustrated." I took him by the shoulders, looked him right in the eyes and said, "Deal with it!"

He didn't understand. Then I explained. Every believer who desperately wants more of God's power and presence in their lives is going to keep pursuing Him. The more they receive, the more they'll want!

The moment you feel satisfied with what we have, the moment you feel that you've "got it," that you've "arrived," you're in trouble. I told this young man, "I made a decision over thirty years ago to pursue the Holy Spirit. I wake up every morning feeling desperate."

People on a pursuit are people who constantly move to new levels of anointing. They are people who are "on the move" into deeper relationship, more authority and increased passion. They are people who impact their world!

If you want anointing, hang around people with anointing. If you have a choice, don't hang around people who sap the life out of you, who sap the faith out of you. Seek out others who are flowing in the river of God.

In my life, with my busy schedule and the schedules of most of my friends, it is hard to meet. But I seek out my friends through e-mail or telephone and receive encouragement and a sense of anointing from them electronically. We give each other good reports. We build each other up. We share anointing with each other.

Elisha received his anointing, not only because he was pursuing it but also because he was *hungry*. There's nothing wrong with wanting more! There is, however, something terribly wrong with saying, "I've got enough." Elisha was hungry. He looked at Elijah and said, "I know you have a special anointing. I know you've done great things. I know you have healed the sick—but I want more than you have. In fact, I want twice as much as you have!"[17]

Sometimes people say to me, "I'd really like you to pray for me to get what you've got." That is scary! If you would be satisfied with having what I have, I wouldn't even bother praying for you. But if you told me, "I could never be satisfied with what you have—I want at least twice as much," that would excite me!

People on a pursuit of the Holy Spirit are some of the busiest people I know. My good friend, Rodney Howard-Browne, was in town preaching a while ago. I wanted to go to one of his meetings. At the time, I was taping television programs, and I was physically so tired, everything in me was begging me to stay home and rest. I knew, however, how refreshing Rodney's meetings are; so despite my weariness, I went.

It turned out that Rodney himself was very tired too. He called me up and asked me to pray for him. He wanted to be refreshed! Afterwards, in the hospitality room, as we were talking about our very heavy schedules, we looked at one another and said, "What can you do? This is what we've been waiting for!"

On another occasion, John and Carol Arnott, who at the time were starting a daily television show, asked me to pray with them before they began taping. A daily show takes a lot of work; it takes a lot out of you. So we prayed. Later, as we were talking about the massive amount of work, John said, "Wouldn't it have been nice if this had all happened about twenty years ago when we were young? However, this is the day! We have been waiting for this day." It's time to go "flat out" and keep on doing, keep on giving, keep on pouring!

We need to be as hungry as Elisha was for the anointing. He received it because he reached out and *took it*! Many of us would have looked at Elijah's coat and said, "Well, that era's over. He's gone." But that mantle represented all that God had done through Elijah—Elisha simply picked it up and wrapped it around himself.

Benny Hinn went to a Kathryn Kuhlman service in 1974. There he saw a woman who had a relationship with the Holy Spirit. To her, the Holy Spirit was not just a doctrine—He was a Friend, a Lover, a Companion. Benny decided in his heart that he wanted the same kind of relationship. He wanted more. So he went after it. He pursued it, got hungry and took it!

Now, imagine Elisha coming back to the banks of the river Jordan wearing the mantle. Second Kings chapter 2 says that fifty men of the sons of the prophets were standing, watching him at a distance. These men were probably thinking, "Elisha hasn't got it. He's no Elijah. Watch, he's going to drown in the river!" As soon as we start moving out with the mantle of healing anointing, people around us will stand back and watch from a distance, looking down at us to say, "Who do they think they are?" Don't let it stop you from pursuing His precious anointing!

When you're in an atmosphere permeated with the presence of God, it's easy to receive the anointing. But living and sustaining that anointing the next day, the next week, the next month, the next year—that is the challenging part. Just like that young man from England, decide today to actively pursue the Holy Spirit!

---

[1] 1 Samuel 16:13.

[2] 1 Samuel 17:15.

[3] 1 Samuel 16:21, ESV.

[4] Daniel 11:32.

[5] 1 Samuel 30:6, KJV.

[6] Psalm 103:3, emphasis added.

[7] Psalm 121:1, KJV.

[8] Psalm 121:2.

[9] 1 Peter 2:10.

[10] 1 Peter 2:9.

[11] Deuteronomy 28:13.

[12] Galatians 4:7.

[13] 2 Corinthians 12:10.

[14] Matthew 16:19, NASB.

[15] 1 John 4:4.

[16] 2 Kings 2:1-14.

[17] 2 Kings 2:9.

Chapter Eight

Are You Going to Do It?

Now, having laid down the principles for healing, I want to share my personal journey with you. A life of continual anointing has many demands.

I had the privilege of attending several services conducted by Kathryn Kuhlman in the early 1970s. She often made this comment, with tears streaming down her face and in her unique manner, "If you want to know how much it costs—if you *really* want to know, let me tell you, it will not cost you something—it will cost you everything!"

On the surface it may seem that people who are in healing ministry have a lot going for them. I must tell you, however, there's a great price to pay. There are so many attacks, so much pressure.

If the Holy Spirit Doesn't Show Up, You're in Trouble!

I appreciate the anointing probably more than anyone, because I know what I am without it! I committed my life to Jesus when I was eighteen years old. It was a wonderful experience! Shortly afterward, when I was filled with the Holy Spirit and spoke in tongues, I felt energized, empowered and free. I felt a fresh passion for God's Word and for Jesus.

A few weeks later, God called me to ministry. That was a totally different experience. God made it very clear. He said, "I'm calling you to preach the gospel."

People often ask me, "How do you know if God is calling you into ministry?" My answer is, "If you don't know, He's not calling you." There was no question in my mind about my calling. The invitation was clear, and my answer was clear too: "No!"

I didn't feel I was being rebellious against His call. It was simply that becoming a preacher wasn't even on my list of things I wanted to do. I was very shy and had difficulty speaking in front of people. What I really wanted to do was to become a funeral director, not a preacher. (It didn't occur to me at the time that I'd be dealing with dead bodies on a daily basis—I just thought about the big black car I'd drive and the nice suit and tie I'd get to wear. I'm so glad God didn't fulfill that desire!)

But I said "no" to God primarily because I felt I had nothing to offer Him or anyone else. All the "successful" ministers I knew of had great abilities and strengths. They were smart, great communicators, well educated, and many of them could play musical instruments and lead worship services with skill. Besides, I thought to myself, "God has enough problems to handle without taking me on as a ministry project!"

In the early years of ministry, I developed a friendship with a man who is good at everything. He looks good, speaks skilfully, sings beautifully, and plays almost any instrument. In spite of my admiration for him, it was hard not to envy him. I thought to myself, "Why do some guys get everything and some guys get nothing?"

This friend called me one day and asked me to meet with him. Both our schedules were so full that we had trouble arranging a mutually suitable time. Finally, he said, "Guess what? I've got my pilot's license and my own plane [one more reason for me to envy him!]. I'll come up and I'll fly you to your next meeting. That will give us time to visit together." So the date was set.

I admired his piloting abilities as he manoeuvred the plane flying through the busy Toronto skies. Once we were outside the city, he put the plane on automatic pilot and took his headphones off. He looked at me and said, "The reason I had to talk to you today was so I could ask you to forgive me. I've always struggled with envy towards you." I was amazed. I thought I had heard wrong.

He continued, "I can have a good meeting with or without God. If my preaching isn't going well, I can go to the piano and start playing. I can sing a song that will touch people's emotions. One way or another, I can get a response out of the congregation. But that's been my problem—I've relied on my abilities. But I look at you and realize that you don't know how to do anything. If the Holy Spirit doesn't show up, you're in trouble. You've got nothing to fall back on! So you rely totally on Him."

It's funny how, when you describe your own inabilities, it sounds different than when someone else does! But he was absolutely right. That was my objection when I first heard God's call to ministry; I had nothing to offer. I didn't know how to do anything. All I had was His anointing.

Since then, I've discovered that when you refuse God's call, that's not the end of the conversation! One night, I stood at the altar in my home church and, with tears in my eyes, said, "God, I don't know why you want me. I feel I can't do anything for you. I feel I've got nothing to offer. All I've got is my life. That's all I've got—so I'll give that to you." I didn't understand at the time, but that's all He needed! When you accept God's invitation, He gives you anointing. And with anointing comes equipping. God loves to use people who "haven't got it" and know they "haven't got it"!

In 1972, when our healing ministry was launched, amazing breakthroughs happened everywhere we went as people experienced healing in their bodies and thousands of souls were swept into His kingdom.

In one of those glorious meetings, a dear friend who had known me for several years witnessed the phenomenon and quipped, "Bill, this *has* to be God. Anyone who knows you knows you're too stupid to do it on your own!" It was meant as a joke, but it really was the truth. God loves to use the foolish to confound the wise.[1] It's not qualifications He looks for, but willingness.

When I finally submitted to God's call to ministry, I knew He had anointed me to preach the gospel. The problem was, nobody wanted to hear what I had to say! I remember Kathryn Kuhlman saying, "If God's called you to preach, you'll preach. If you have to live on bread and water, you'll preach. If you have to stand on street corners, you'll preach."

That is exactly what I began doing. Gwen and I lived just outside of Toronto and heard that *Teen Challenge*[2] was desperate for workers. Every day after work, she and I would rush downtown to meet with the leaders and other volunteers at *Teen Challenge*, pray with them and go out into the streets. That's where I started ministering to broken and hurting people.

The following year I married my sweetheart and began studying for the ministry at a Bible college. I heard that every week the college leadership sent students to minister and represent the school at different churches, so I asked to be included.

The coordinators asked me if I played any musical instrument or could sing. I answered, "No, I preach." They replied enthusiastically, "Wonderful! We need preachers. Give us a list of all the churches you've preached at and all the pastors you have worked with so that we can check your references." I replied, "Well, I haven't actually preached anywhere yet. I've preached on the streets."

They told me that they would only send people with experience. "But that's why I came to Bible college!" I thought. How could I get the needed experience if I wasn't permitted to do anything?

Then I heard about a group of students that travelled out to an Indian reservation every week to conduct house meetings. They allowed me to join, so I began preaching to the little groups that gathered for services on that reservation. I fell in love with these precious native people. It was in those humble little meetings that I got "hooked" on native ministry, which now encompasses Arctic Canada and Arctic Russia.

Actually, the first miracle I ever participated in took place on that reservation. The meetings were held in Mrs. Gray's house. One day, after I finished preaching, talking about Jesus' greatness and power, Mrs. Gray asked me to pray for her little boy who had boils under his arm. Infection had spread, and it looked painful and nasty. I laid hands on him and asked Jesus to heal him. At that point, it never occurred to me to check to see if anything had happened. Our group just said "God bless you" and left.

When we returned the following week, out of courtesy, I asked Mrs. Gray how her son was doing. She answered, "He's fine."

"But how are his boils?" I asked.

"He doesn't have any boils," she replied.

I couldn't believe she had forgotten so easily. "Remember when we were here last week," I said, "you asked us to pray for his boils."

"Yes," she responded, looking at me curiously.

"So, how is he?" I asked again.

Once again she replied, "He doesn't have any boils."

"What do you mean? What happened?" I asked.

She replied, "You prayed last Sunday; then you left. So I checked under his arm, and all the boils and infection were gone. God healed him." As simple as that!

I was stunned! It had never occurred to me that the Lord would actually answer my prayer! I'd been conditioned to be "cautious" about expecting a miracle. In my head I knew God *could* heal, but I really didn't think He actually *would*!

Up until that day, I had never seen a real miracle take place. There wasn't a mark on the boy's body! Mrs. Gray had two boys close in age and appearance, and one of my fellow students came up with a brilliant explanation—she switched kids! But we soon came to realize that God had indeed healed this child. We were ecstatic!

These precious First Nation people had simple faith. As soon as we prayed, they were confident that God would heal the little boy. But we, the Bible school students, who had come to teach them that "God is big, and can do anything," were surprised!

It was a humbling experience, as I realized how shallow my faith was. As we made our way home that night, I prayed in the car, "Lord I don't want 'white man's faith' any more. Give me 'Indian faith,' that takes you at Your Word." Something happened in my heart that day. Now, when I pray for people, I believe I'm praying with "Indian faith"!

Ever since I was young, I've wanted to see people healed. I remember watching Oral Roberts on television with amazement, and thought, "If God really is as big as people say He is, why don't miracles happen all the time?" Later on, when I became a pastor after graduating from Bible college, this desire to help people, the compassion in my heart, grew even more. But in the early years of my ministry I saw very few results.

Have You Been Waiting for Me?

A few years passed, and one night, as I was listening to the radio on my way home from the little church I pastored in Quebec, I heard an unusual voice of a woman saying, "Hellooo there. Have you been wai-ting for me?"

That unique, deliberate voice was my introduction to Kathryn Kuhlman. On the program, I heard one testimony after another from people who were receiving healing. Doctors in attendance were verifying the results right there on the air.

When I came home I told my wife, "Gwen, I don't know anything about this person. She sounds strange, but miracles are happening." From that day on, every night Gwen and I would go sit in the car (there was no reception inside the house) at nine o'clock and listen.

Around that same time my wife became very ill and was hospitalized for a week to undergo tests and treatment. She was released with strict orders to have complete bedrest. We had three little children at the time, and we'd sent them off to my parents' home in Brampton, Ontario, near Toronto, for my mom to care for while Gwen was in hospital. I was about to call Mom to ask her if she could continue looking after them for a while, when Gwen said, "Take me to Brampton. I want to get my kids." There was no arguing with her. She lay on the back seat of the car and I began the seven-hour drive to Brampton.

On the way, at nine o'clock, we tuned into Kathryn's radio program, and once again heard the familiar voice ask, "Hellooo there. Have you been wai-ting for me?" But that night, the program consisted only of worship and praise, not healing testimonies. I was, to say the least, very disappointed. The entire radio show that night was the sound of people worshipping God. As we listened, God's presence filled our car to the point that I literally began to shake—and Gwen was totally healed by the power of God!

On the Bus

Shortly after Gwen's miraculous healing, we moved to pastor a church in Beachburg, a little community in eastern Ontario. We discovered that every week busloads of people would travel twelve hours one way, to Pittsburgh to attend Friday morning miracle services conducted by Kathryn Kuhlman.

This tradition had begun after Ken May, a Presbyterian man who had been diagnosed with terminal cancer, made a visit to Pittsburgh to say goodbye to his daughter who lived there. On the way, he read a book someone had given him, called *I Believe in Miracles*, written by Kathryn Kuhlman. In Pittsburgh, he found out about Kathryn Kuhlman's weekly meetings at the local Presbyterian church. He decided to go.

Before he could even get into the church, as he stood on the steps, he was healed of cancer. When he got back home, the same doctors who told him he was going to die confirmed that he didn't have cancer any more!

The following week he returned to Pittsburgh with a carload of friends who needed healing. One lady was healed of multiple sclerosis during that trip. In the following weeks, greater numbers began to make the journey. Soon Ken decided to quit his job and go full-time into bus ministry! Every time he heard of anyone in the area who was sick, he would go and visit them, telling them what had happened to him. They would then buy tickets and get on the bus to go to Pittsburgh with him.

When I heard about these pilgrimages, I began wondering why everyone felt they had to travel so far to experience the power of God. One or two other ministers in the area, threatened by the numbers taking these trips, complained that if these same people came to their churches with the same faith, they could receive the same thing. It seemed to make sense to me, yet very little ever happened in any of their meetings, or in mine.

In the meantime, a few people began dropping seeds of suspicion in my heart about Kathryn Kuhlman, warning me that there were some questionable things about her that I wasn't aware of, and that, after all, she wasn't even Pentecostal! And although I had witnessed my wife's healing with my own eyes, under the influence of these seeds of doubt, I began to develop a critical attitude toward Kathryn.

I knew that every week a minister would be asked to join the group going to Pittsburgh, to serve as "bus pastor." One night, I received a call, asking me to replace the scheduled pastor on the bus because he had taken ill. The organizers had contacted all the other pastors they knew of, but no one could go. I was their last resort.

I was torn. I'd become critical of Kathryn, like some of my peers, but I was also curious. So, the next morning, I was on the bus going to this meeting led by a woman who was "not even Pentecostal"! As I looked around the bus, I thought, "These people must all be 'troublemakers,' running all over the country for a thrill, instead of settling down in their own churches."

I didn't know at the time that many of them never attended church, or were nominal Christians at best, who had come desperate for a miracle. I specifically remember a four-year-old girl whose parents had been told by doctors that she would never walk. Her little legs hung rubbery and useless as she travelled with her mother. I prayed, "Oh God, no matter what else happens, if no one else is healed, please heal this little girl."

Following a short night's rest, we made our way to the Presbyterian church where the meeting was to take place. I was amazed as hundreds stood for hours on the steps, in the freezing March drizzle, early in the morning, waiting for the doors to open. When they did, a wave of bodies literally pushed me inside.

I found a seat about three-quarters of the way back in the auditorium. With my critical attitude, I determined not to enjoy any part of that meeting. I didn't feel like talking to anyone. But the woman sitting beside me struck up a conversation with me, telling me that she was a Roman

Catholic and had driven all the way from southern Ontario on her own.

She was very pleased when she discovered I was a Pentecostal minister. She had never been to a meeting of this nature before and felt assured that, with my expertise, I'd be able to explain things to her. Little did she know that the atmosphere was just as foreign to me!

I asked her, "Why have you come here all the way from Ontario?"

She answered, "I need a miracle."

When people need a miracle—when they are desperate—they will come. When they hear that God is using someone to heal people, they will come. They aren't going to argue doctrine or debate church practices. They're looking for something that works!

At that moment the great organ sounded, and the spotlight lit up. Out walked Kathryn Kuhlman, with her striking red hair and flowing white dress, onto the stage. As she led us in worship, her long bony arms waved up and down gracefully like a butterfly, and she seemed to float across the stage.

In her opening remarks she said, "I'm the most ordinary person in the world." With my critical attitude, looking at her riveting appearance and dramatic entrance, I thought, "No you're not! There's nothing 'ordinary' about you!"

Then she prayed, "Jesus, don't let them see me—let them see You." In my mind, I scoffed, "If you don't want to be seen, turn off the spotlight! Wear a black dress!"

Despite my determination to be critical, I began feeling overwhelmed by the presence of God. Kathryn began praying for people. As she laid hands on them, they fell to the floor, one after another. The Catholic woman beside me grabbed my arm and asked, "What's she doing to them?"

I patted her hand and said, "It's all right; this is just the power of God." She had no idea that I was the one who wanted to grab *her* arm and ask her what was happening! I had never in my life seen anything like that.

As soon as I uttered the words, "This is just the power of God," I felt the Holy Spirit touch me and say, "Yes, this is my power, and you've never seen it. You've had a form of godliness and denied my power." I began to weep.

The Catholic woman asked me if I was okay. I answered, "No."

She said, "Can I help you?"

I said, "No, no one can."

And I wept. I wept because I realized at that moment that I didn't really *know* the Holy Spirit at all. I had committed my life to Jesus, been baptized in the Holy Spirit, spoke in tongues and claimed to know the Holy Spirit. But all of a sudden I came to the realization that, even though I had been introduced to Him, met Him and received a gift from Him, I didn't *know* Him. All the knowledge I had accumulated at Bible college was just doctrine. It was all in my head, not in my heart. There was no passion, no life. But that night, I made a decision to spend the rest of my life pursuing the Holy Spirit.

That morning, even though I didn't have any contact with Kathryn Kuhlman, my life was changed forever. On the bus ride home, however, we began to realize that nobody on our bus had been healed, in spite of all the miracles we had witnessed in the meeting.

The bus driver challenged me, "If God is real, why didn't He heal that little girl?"

"I don't know," I answered, "but we saw some amazing things happen." I sat in my seat, reviewing in my mind all I had seen and felt. Pretty soon, I began to get sleepy and put my seat in the reclining position to have a nap.

Suddenly things began to happen. A lady who knew nothing about the Baptism of the Holy Spirit began speaking in tongues. It was a novelty to most on the bus, and they gathered around to listen. Soon, one after another began reporting that God was healing them right there on the bus. As they came forward to testify over the bus's microphone, God's power came on them, and they began falling into the slushy aisles! It soon occurred to us that we needed a "catcher." We were experiencing a full-blown miracle service!

Suddenly we heard a cry from the back of the bus. I turned to see the little four-year-old girl, whose legs had been useless, walking up the aisle!

The bus driver began to sob, as he looked in his rear-view mirror and saw the little girl walking. For the first time, he saw the reality of God's power for himself. Before the end of the trip, he committed his life to Christ.

About thirty years after that memorable night, I received an interesting e-mail. It read, "I just want to let you know that what happened on that bus in 1972 is still happening. I'm an ordained minister in a Pentecostal organization. I'm an executive member in our fellowship. In every service I conduct, I pray for the sick, and the sick are being healed. My dad was the bus driver on your trip to Pittsburgh, and what happened on that bus in 1972 is still happening." It was just one more reminder of the impact that the anointing makes.

You Pursue; They'll Come

Beachburg, where we were pastoring, is a very small but "nice" village with a population of 540. The church was "nice" and the congregation was "nice." We had a "nice," uneventful life, with our four "nice" little children and a "nice" little parsonage. Everything was "nice"—predictable, but "nice."

Shortly before my trip to Pittsburgh, I had been invited to do an evangelistic crusade just a few miles from where we lived. The crusade was held in the "Little Brown Church," which held only about fifty people. (It got its name for three reasons: it was *little*, it was *brown,* and it was a *church*!)

Even that small place looked empty that night. Only a handful of people showed up, and they all looked miserable. I preached a fiery salvation message and gave an altar call. Nobody moved. They just sat there. The following night, I preached on healing and invited the few people who did show up to come forward if they needed prayer. Again, no one moved. No one would even let me pray for them. The third and last night of the crusade, I preached on the baptism of the Holy Spirit, because I thought they needed joy. Again, nobody came forward for prayer. Nobody wanted the joy of the Spirit!

The crusade was a bust. I had done my best (note, "*I*" had done my best) and nothing happened. And I blamed it all on the people. Obviously, *they* had a problem.

But on that bus, coming back from Pittsburgh, I hadn't asked for a healing ministry. I had decided simply to pursue the Holy Spirit, and things began to happen!

I spent the entire next day, Saturday, on my face before God, repenting and praying, "I just have to know You. Nothing else matters."

On Sunday morning, as I went to the platform, I couldn't even stand behind the pulpit. I thought, "Holy Spirit, I've taken centre stage for too long. You take over."

I stood to one side of the platform and blubbered through the service, repenting to these dear people who had endured my cocky attitude and shallow experience. I didn't care what people thought.

At the end of the service, several people came up to me and told me they had been healed that morning. I had prayed for these same people many times, and they had never been healed. This morning, however, while I stood aside crying and praying, they were healed!

Every desire you may have for ministry can only be fulfilled when you stop pursuing *it* and start pursuing *Him*—the third person of the Trinity—the wonderful Holy Spirit.

Many people were healed during that Sunday morning service, and I was overwhelmed. I sent Gwen home with the children while I stayed all afternoon, lying on my face on the floor of my office, seeking the Lord. As I walked out to begin the evening service, I was shocked to see the auditorium packed. Before this, only a handful showed up for our evening services.

The place was electrified with the presence of God. I simply invited the Holy Spirit to come, and miracles began to take place. That night more people responded to the salvation invitation and received Christ than I had seen in total during my previous six years of ministry!

Many of those in attendance didn't even know why they had come. Something just told them that they needed to show up. No advertising had gone out, and we'd made no announcements or promotion of any kind. I had simply started pursuing the Holy Spirit, and immediately the power of God began to move. I found out that night that I didn't need to be good at anything other than the pursuit of the Holy Spirit.

Over the following months, hundreds arrived in Beachburg every week to witness and receive miracles. Most were people who had never understood the gospel message before. Week after week, scores crowded to the front, giving their lives to Christ, and many more received the Holy Spirit's power. It truly was an amazing move of God that launched us into a nationwide healing ministry and has taken us around the world.

An Endless Pursuit

The difference between the Church today and the book of Acts Church is their attitude towards the Holy Spirit. The early Church never treated the Holy Spirit as a controversial doctrine, but rather, exactly as they treated Jesus—as their Friend, their Companion and Counsellor.

Not long ago, I was sound asleep in my hotel room when I suddenly felt the Holy Spirit waking me up. I sat up, expecting a revelation or a message, but nothing came. It happened one more time. This time, I asked the Holy Spirit what He wanted to tell me. I felt Him responding, "I noticed that you were busy all day and didn't have a lot of time. I woke you up so you could spend time with me."

This isn't doctrine or theology I'm talking about. I am talking about *relationship*.

The Holy Spirit wants to put His loving arms around us. He wants to be *with* us and *in* us.

I had wasted years pursuing results. My pursuit of the Holy Spirit began in 1972 and continues to this day. And I'm constantly discovering more. Still today, I say to the Holy Spirit, "I want to know You. The more I see of You, the more I want to see." The decision I made so many years ago was the best decision I have ever made. I am pursuing Him. And His power just keeps flowing.

The Holy Spirit wants to be pursued!

In 1963, I met a beautiful young lady. She was one of the on-air personalities of a Christian radio show for youth that aired every Saturday. I had been invited to share my testimony. (I didn't even know what a "testimony" was, since I wasn't a committed Christian, but everyone thought I was, so I was chosen.)

The young lady's name was Gwen. She was really cute. As soon as I met her, I decided I wanted to get to know her. How do you get to know someone? You go after them. So I'd ask Gwen, "Do you want to go for a walk? Do you want to talk? Can I drive you home after church? Can I take you out to A&W?" She agreed each time, and that was the beginning of our relationship. The more time we spent together, the better I got to know her.

If you want to get to know someone, you spend time with him or her. It is not that difficult. A while ago I asked Gwen, "Did you know that I was pursuing you?" She answered, "Did you know that *I* was pursuing *you?*"

It's so much easier to pursue someone who is pursuing you! The Holy Spirit wants to be pursued *and* is pursuing *you*. If you draw near to Him, He will draw near to you.

My encounter with the Holy Spirit in Pittsburgh, and the beginning of my relationship with Him, took place in 1972, yet it's as real today as it was then. In fact, in some ways it's even more real. I came out of that place not knowing what had happened, not knowing that my life and ministry were about to totally change. I just knew that I had met the most wonderful Person in the world.

Unfortunately, many believers think that they know

Him, but they really don't. I've even met traditional Pentecostal pastors who are breaking under the strain of ministry because they're trying to process information about the Holy Spirit without knowing Him. When you renew your relationship with the Holy Spirit, God restores the delight of ministry, and truly His yoke becomes easy and His burden becomes light.[3]

You must find time alone just to listen to Him. And you'll be amazed that if you listen, He'll talk to you! Prayer no longer remains a one-way conversation—it becomes communion.

A very dear friend of mine was a Greek professor at one of our leading Christian colleges. He is a great preacher and has trained many young people for ministry. This man went to China a few years ago to teach some seminars for the local believers in the underground Church. Before one of his sessions, someone pointed out that all the people sitting in the front row had at one point raised someone from the dead! My friend was humbled and intimidated. How could he teach the Word to all these true "apostles"?

This man was deeply impacted by the way the Chinese Christians prayed. He told me that he met a little four-foot-tall Chinese woman who took him under her wing and taught him how to pray. The believers would begin their day at four o'clock, every morning. First, they prayed aloud. Then they prayed for each other. Afterwards, they had a time of praise and celebration, and all this time they stayed on their knees. Then, for three hours, they didn't talk; they just listened. At nine o'clock, they got up and went to work.

Perhaps that's why they were able to raise the dead—they listened to God. They had a special relationship with the Holy Spirit.

I've met some believers who sense that God has called them to a specific ministry, but many of them are waiting for certain things to happen before they answer the call. For example, I know someone who was a missionary, but the mission board of his denomination decided to take him out of the field due to lack of finances. He was offered a different mission field, but he refused. He returned to Canada, very bitter, and blaming the board for his lack of fulfillment. He has now stopped going to church and is involved in secular business.

We are all going to stand before God and give an account for how we responded to His call. I just don't think that when we stand before Him it will be enough to say, "Well, the mission board wouldn't send me. My denomination wouldn't finance me."

Jonathan Goforth was a Canadian who lived around the turn of the twentieth century. God called him to China. He obeyed and began ministering to the Chinese in the face of bitter and dangerous opposition. A while later, his mission board decided to send him to Korea, but Jonathan Goforth knew that he was called to work in China. So, despite the fact that all his financial support was withdrawn, he remained in China, and revival began. There are reports that he baptized over five thousand Chinese soldiers who came to Christ in one day. Today, many Chinese Christians attribute their nationwide revival to one man, Jonathan Goforth, who stayed against all odds and carried out the mission to which God had called him.[4]

If God is calling you to do something, then He is certainly able to equip and prepare you for what He has for you. And as you develop your relationship with the Holy Spirit, nothing will keep you from fulfilling His call on your life. He will sustain you in the most impossible circumstances and give you joy while you do it!

There are evangelists here in Canada who aren't accomplishing anything because their denominations don't support them. They are bitter and unfruitful. God always makes a way for ministry, but sometimes we have to be aggressive and "go for it"! God is big enough to fulfill the vision that He has put in our hearts.

Has God put a dream or a vision in your heart? No matter how busy you are, I encourage you to take time to listen to Him. But you must be still to hear Him.

The Ottawa Lay School of Theology runs a program every year for lay people who want to learn about theology. The program is sponsored by Anglican, Presbyterian and United churches and has been very well received.

Several years ago, a friend of mine, a United church minister who was one of the leaders at the school, called to ask me to be a guest lecturer at the school. I was a little surprised, because the school isn't Pentecostal. He explained that the specific course he wanted me to teach was on "Prayer Concerning Physical Healing" and that the usual lecturer didn't feel qualified to teach it.

I agreed, but later, the more I thought about it, the more uncomfortable I became with my decision. I thought, "These people are not Pentecostal, and they're not going to like me or believe anything I say." But I had made a commitment and couldn't back out.

As the date of the lecture drew closer, I became more and more nervous. Finally, the day arrived and I went to the school. My friend and some of the other leaders met me. They were rather excited, because an unusually large number of people had enrolled in my class.

They took me in and introduced me. Then they explained the structure of the evening to me: I was allotted a certain amount of time to teach, followed by a short break; then there would be a question period. I looked at the crowd. It seemed to me that they were glaring at me! They didn't look very happy, and I really didn't feel like answering any questions they might have. I assumed they would attack my theology or, at the very least, challenge me.

I reluctantly began. I talked about what God had done in my family's life—the healings and miracles we had experienced. I spoke longer than I was supposed to, hoping there would be no time left for questions, but the host told me they were very flexible and could stay later in order to take advantage of the question period.

Immediately after we came back from the break, a woman put up her hand. "Mr. Prankard, we really need to thank you." I could breathe again! She continued, "About a year ago, my mother was dying of cancer. I brought her to one of your meetings, and God totally healed her. The doctors were amazed. My mother is doing well to this day, and this is the first chance I've had to share this with you."

Another lady stood up and said, "I was healed in one of your meetings." She went on to tell everyone what God had done. I was beginning to feel a little more at ease. Then a few people had some very intelligent questions, and I did my best to answer them.

As I was trying to wrap up, I noticed a lady at the back of the room, waving her hand madly in the air. She looked like a troublemaker to me, but I had no choice and said, "We'll take one more question."

She stood up and said, "Are you going to do it?" I had no idea what she was talking about. I asked her what she meant, and she said, “The healing thing—are you going to do it?”

I heard myself reply, “Of course we’re going to do it! You don’t think I’d just come and talk about it, do you?” My goal had been to get out of there as easily as possible, but this lady’s question made me stand back and watch, then listen to myself…I had said it, and now I had to do it!

I had no idea what I was going to do next. I felt absolutely no anointing. Then, once again, I heard myself say, “If you have a problem in your body, put your hand on that area.” I really didn’t expect anyone in that crowd to respond, because they were all dignified, conservative people. So I closed my eyes real tight and prayed a very long prayer! I thought if I prayed long enough, they might all leave.

Finally, I opened my eyes. I was shocked! Almost everyone had their hand somewhere on their bodies. Several people had tears running down their cheeks. I felt the presence of God. One lady said, “I’ve just been healed.” One after another, they began to share. To this day, most of them don’t know that I had no intention of praying for them that night or that it hadn’t even occurred to me to minister to them.

At some point somebody will ask you, after you’ve joined in all the songs about how big God is, taken all the classes about His will for healing, read all the Scriptures about God’s promises: “Are you going to do it?”

The devil doesn’t care how much knowledge you’ve accumulated. He does care however, when you say, “Yes! I’m going to do it.” He may even bring out the “big guns” against you! He may oppose you relentlessly. But take it as a compliment and declare, “Greater is He that is in me than he that is in the world."[5] Take the authority the Lord has entrusted you with, and do it!

These are great days of opportunity. Are you going to do it?

People are more open and attuned to the supernatural. Are you going to do it?

People aren't looking for religion, but they are looking for power. Are you going to do it?

Are you going to do it?

---

[1] 1 Corinthians 1:27.

[2] Teen Challenge is a ministry to troubled youth, founded by Reverend David Wilkerson in New York City.

[3] Matthew 11:30.

[4] Janet and Geoff Benge, *Jonathan Goforth—An Open Door in China* (Seattle, WA: YWAM Publishing, 2001). Don Young "Jonathan Goforth: China's Greatest Evangelist," *The Pentecostal Testimony*, January 1991.

[5] See 1 John 4:4.